Working on the Inside

Working on the Inside

The Spiritual Life through the Eyes of Actors

RETTA BLANEY

A SHEED & WARD BOOK

ROWMAN & LITTLEFIELD PUBLISHERS, INC.

Lanham • Boulder • New York • Oxford

A SHEED & WARD BOOK

ROWMAN & LITTLEFIELD PUBLISHERS, INC.

Published in the United States of America
by Rowman & Littlefield Publishers, Inc.

A wholly owned subsidiary of the Rowman & Littlefield Publishing Group
4501 Forbes Boulevard, Suite 200, Lanham, Maryland 20706
www.rowmanlittlefield.com

PO Box 317
Oxford
OX2 9RU, UK

All biblical quotes taken from the New Revised Standard Version and the
New American Bible.

British Library Cataloguing in Publication Information Available

Library of Congress Cataloging-in-Publication Data

Blaney, Retta.
    Working on the inside : the spiritual life through the eyes of actors /
Retta Blaney.
        p. cm.
    Includes bibliographical references.
    ISBN 0-7425-3319-0 (pbk. : alk. paper)
    1. Christian biography—United States. 2. Actors—Religious life—
United States. 3. Jewish actors—United States—Biography. I. Title.
BR1702.B55 2003
277.3'083'0922—dc21   2003006156

Printed in the United States of America

♾™ The paper used in this publication meets the minimum requirements of
American National Standard for Information Sciences—Permanence of Paper
for Printed Library Materials, ANSI/NISO Z39.48-1992.

For my father,
from whom I received my spiritual nature

Contents

Acknowledgments

I thank my publisher at Sheed & Ward, Jeremy Langford, for having faith in my project and allowing me the freedom to let it be what it would be, and I thank the Rev. James Martin, S.J., for bringing us together.

Thank you once again, Jon Furay, for reading my contract and advising me.

Thank you, Merwin Goldsmith, not only for the terrific interview, but for graciously offering to take my book publicity photos as well. What a thoughtful person!

And thank you to the congregation and staff of St. Clement's Episcopal Church for allowing me to photograph their wonderful space.

I am grateful to the following people for leading me to so many great actors and clergy members: the Rev. Daniel Berrigan, S.J.; the Rev. Barbara C. Crafton; Msgr. Michael C. Crimmins; Dr. Emil Dansker; Sr. Mary Dowd, OSU; Sr. Mary Gallagher, SC; Rabbi Loraine Heller; the Rev. Kate Kinney; the Rev. Dr. Peregrine L. Murphy; the Very Rev. Harry H. Pritchett; and Diane Snyder.

Thank you, Fr. Erno Diaz, for the use of the cozy little parlor on the second floor of St. Malachy's rectory. That space, right in the heart of the theatre district, was a godsend to me for doing many of these interviews.

And thank you, Stephanie Fischman and Peter Smith, for always being available to me with computer assistance. Your Luddite friend appreciates all the help.

Introduction

THE IDEA for this book came from my many years of interviewing stage actors. Time and again they brought up the need for a spiritual life. I have covered many beats in my life—politics, education, and business to name three—but I never encountered anyone in those fields who spoke about spiritual matters in relationship to their careers. If they had spiritual lives, which I'm sure plenty of them did, they didn't speak about them. It was as if they had compartmentalized their lives, reserving weekdays for work and weekends for religious thoughts and practices. I found something quite different in covering the performing arts. A great many actors think of their work as spiritual, especially when they are doing theatre. As Edward Herrmann says: "If you're lucky enough to have the arts as your work, you become part of the spiritual life." It was an actor who inadvertently provided me with the title for this book. Like most people in the field, he had had his share of barrenness and fruitfulness in his career, so I asked him how he handled the ups and downs. He said: "I work on the inside." When I asked him to explain, he said: "I've got to breathe, pray, meditate, and focus on the day."

Interestingly, the spiritual life is what actors are seldom asked about. As I read their clip files in the New York Public Library for the

Performing Arts, I learned about their past performances, their financial and personal lives, including intimate details, but I didn't learn about their inner selves. It seemed no one was asking the questions I wanted to ask: Do you pray? How do you pray? What do you pray for? My instincts told me actors would want to talk about these things because the spiritual life is important to them and because by talking about it they would reveal a side of themselves the public rarely, if ever, hears about. So I requested interviews, got them, asked the questions, and got answers. Yes, actors pray, in gratitude and for direction. As Vanessa Williams told me: "When I'm alone I pray before sleep . . . I ask God to protect my family and friends and ask for good health. I never pray 'I want this part'; I pray to be guided and then it gets done." And I heard over and over a deep trust—faith— that God had given them their gifts and that God would provide them with the opportunity to use those gifts. Kristin Chenoweth put it well when she said: "Like most actors, I have my insecurities. My prayer with the Lord every day is not to take things personally. I say, 'Okay, you gave me this gift. Help me not to doubt it.'"

Working on this book was a blessing in my life, leading me to growth, healing, and transformation, and it is my hope, and that of many of those interviewed here, that others will be helped as well. Actors can offer great wisdom, wisdom they've learned through probing the depths of emotions in performing their roles, as well as by living such precarious lives. They have to learn how to stay grounded, which is why Bertilla Baker's primary prayer is for faith. "Actors are so in touch with that because we have so much uncertainty in our careers. To be a performing artist is to stand with one foot over the cliff at all times." From their faith-producing experiences, they can offer us inspiration, and they can turn those experiences into performances that help us transcend the difficulties in our lives. "There's an erosion of faith," Liam Neeson said. "People don't know what to believe anymore. Actors can give a focus. They can help show another facet of life."

The ten chapters in this book represent different elements of the universal spiritual life, considered from actors' perspective and experience, but these elements also have histories and traditions in organized religion, which is why I interviewed Jewish and Christian clergy for the end of each chapter. I selected these spiritual categories based on earlier interviews, the interviews that through the years made me want to write this book. Actors didn't necessarily use these names, but what they described were spiritual elements. People talked of the need to stay true to themselves, to be grounded and not get lost in a role; that's self-knowledge. Actors regularly talk of the importance of being "in the moment," which in the spiritual world is the idea of being present. And, of course, the faith in their gifts that keeps them going. As the chapters began to take shape, I discovered the actors and the religious "authorities," even though they came from different backgrounds and had different lives, shared similar thoughts. This isn't surprising since theatre and worship can both offer comfort and transformation, but it was interesting to hear the connection voiced repeatedly. It was almost as if the two groups were in dialogue with each other. Merwin Goldsmith offered one explanation, saying that anyone accustomed to religious rituals and their symbolism is especially open to an acting career, particularly someone who has participated in those rituals as an altar server or student cantor. "A preponderance of actors have had religious backgrounds," he said. "Anybody with a religious upbringing can make an easy transfer from religious practice to theatrical practice. You have an understanding of ritual."

The universality of these spiritual elements also was obvious in the comments from the Jewish and Christian religious leaders, who expressed similar thoughts in chapter after chapter. As Dudu Fisher said: "The God of the Muslims, Christians, and Jews is the same God. There's no difference between Gods." And in many ways, there's no difference between all of us, Jews and Christians, actors and those of us who watch them act. We need faith to carry on, we need to listen for direction, and we need a sense of community, of belonging. As Richard Costa put it, "Without a spiritual life I'd be so scattered I wouldn't know where to go."

I am grateful to these actors and clergy members who invited me into their homes, their dressing rooms, their parish houses and offices, or who came to the rectory at St. Malachy's to meet me, a total stranger to most of them, to share such intimate details of their inner lives. I keep them in my prayers, and I pray this book will find its way into the hands of all those out there who also want to work on the inside. I know this will happen because, like the actors, I believe the God who gives the gifts will provide the way.

Faith

Let me hear of your steadfast love in the morning,
for in you I put my trust.
Teach me the way I should go, for to you I lift up my soul.
~PSALM 143:8

And I know
If I'll only be true
To this glorious quest
That my heart
Will lie peaceful and calm
When I'm laid to my rest.
~JOE DARION, *Man of La Mancha*

IT TAKES A LOT of faith to be an actor. Whether it's in God, a less defined higher power, or themselves, faith is as essential as talent for actors because even the best show closes, and they are again out of work, holding themselves out for approval, only, more often than not, to face rejection. As the Rev. Joseph A. Kelly, S.J., parochial vicar of St. Malachy's/The Actors' Chapel, puts it, many are called, few are called back, and only one is chosen.

An element of faith also is involved for those who go to the secular temples we call theatres. We trust we will find some truths for our lives, or simply be lifted out of our worlds, just as we are lifted out of everyday concerns in worship services. Theatregoers have faith in the actors, the priests in the ritual that is theatre, and actors work hard to reward that faith. For many the way to do it is through developing their own close relationship with God.

"You can pick out the artists in the world by their spiritual quality," says singer and actor Jeanne Beauvais, who has relied on faith to sustain her through more than a half century in show business, first in the theatre and now in her classical cabaret performances. She considers St. Jude her patron and prays to him privately and before his statue at St. Malachy's, New York's Roman Catholic ministry to the performing arts community. "That St. Jude has been saving my life so many times. When you're alone you need the saints, all the saints."

Beauvais's studio apartment at Carnegie Hall looks like a backstage dressing room that also serves as a theatre museum and home. Clothes and costumes hang from partitioning screens, in front of which colorful hat boxes are stacked higher than the five-foot three-inch singer. Black and white posters picturing Beauvais as a pretty young woman advertise performances from decades ago, and folders overflow with reviews and production shots from plays long closed. In one photo she wrestles with Shirley Jones while Jack Cassidy looks on. (Offstage, though, they were friends and she sang at their wedding.) Another photo is of an actor with whom she never performed but whom she got to know fairly well, Marlon Brando, who was her next-door neighbor in Carnegie Hall early in his career. For furniture she has four chairs from Row D in the orchestra and four box seats, acquired when

Carnegie Hall was renovated in 1986. "Everybody else has regular furniture," she says. But just to prove she actually lives in the midst of all this theatre memorabilia, a daybed juts out from under the grand piano. Beauvais has many stories of her life onstage and shares them with great flourish. Through them all she weaves stories of the faith that carried her through. "If you're with God, if you really, really believe, it's almost as if you're wafted through the evil," she says.

That strong faith which has wafted her through life has been with her since she was a child growing up Catholic in France. When she was sick on Sunday, she never told her mother because she didn't want to be stopped from going to church. "That was early theatre for me. I had an early, real love for the Church."

When she was ten, she went to her parish priest and told him she wanted to be a singer. He steered her toward the church choir, where she was allowed to solo. The priest told her to "keep your dream and one day you will find it." She began praying to St. Jude because she had heard he was the patron saint of the impossible. She prayed for five years but saw no results, so she "gave up in the right way," telling God and St. Jude that if they didn't want a performing career for her, she would stop seeking it. The next day she was asked to sing with a group of girls on tour. "I left home and never went back."

Since that time she has performed on Broadway, appearing in the original cast of *The King and I* and the revival of *The Boyfriend*; has toured every state except South Dakota; and has sung at Carnegie Hall, in London, Mexico, Iceland, Greenland, islands in the South Pacific, and throughout Europe. Specializing now in French classical interpretations, she sings to sold-out audiences at New York cabarets.

She also has sung at several New York churches through the years, but now considers St. Malachy's home. She was lured there originally by the 4 A.M. Sunday Mass, which the parish offered years ago as a way of attracting the theatrical community. She would finish a performance and head to the Gothic church on Forty-ninth Street, often bringing others with her. "I dragged so many musicians to that church."

Now she is a lector at St. Malachy's and is also called upon to perform, such as at an Easter Vigil when she was asked to play God. Playing God can be a daunting task, but she reached back into her showbiz experience and recalled Yul Brynner, with whom she had appeared in *The King and I*, talking about the importance of making a psychological gesture, which he did when he forgot a line. He would raise a finger majestically to hold the audience's attention until the line came to him. Beauvais hadn't forgotten her lines that Holy Saturday, but she included the psychological gesture anyway. She stretched out her arm and said, "Let there be light," and she had everyone's attention.

Merging the worlds of faith and performance comes naturally to Beauvais. It's a practice she has carried on throughout her career, and she shares many stories of its success. Like the time when she was in her mid-thirties and scheduled to sing in a major recital in London. It couldn't have been a worse time. Her voice teacher had just died and she had a cold, although she wouldn't go to the doctor because she didn't want her manager to find out and pull her from the program. To her, a concert is "a spiritual moment in time," and she didn't want to forgo this one.

After getting through the first song in a passable fashion, she began praying to God and St. Jude while taking her bow. "I said: 'God, you've got to help me. I cannot do this alone.'" Then she opened her mouth to sing, full of confidence, and her prayers were answered. "I never sang that song, somebody else did. I don't know whether it was God or St. Jude or my dead voice teacher."

Critics praised her performance; one said she sounded as if she were "flying over the footlights." When she finally went to the doctor the next day, he told her it was impossible to sing in that condition. But she had. "You ask for the impossible and you get it. That's why I believe."

She continued to pray to St. Jude and even got others believing in the patron saint of the impossible. While touring with the After

Dinner Opera Company in Europe, she impressed the Jewish director, Richard Flusser, with her faith. Seeing that she went to church every Sunday no matter where the company was, he made sure she had a car to take her. And he began to believe in her prayers to St. Jude. Since the performance schedule was only supposed to include the Edinburgh Festival and a concert in London, he suggested the company adopt St. Jude as its patron. Then they began getting additional bookings, one at a time, all over Europe.

"I've been wafted everywhere," she says, summing up her career. "I'm not famous in the way big movie stars are, but I'm famous in my field. I make my audiences happy and I'm happy."

Strong faith is also at the core of Dudu Fisher's life and work; in fact, he doesn't know how anyone in the performing arts can survive without it. "If you really don't believe there's somebody pulling strings up there and there is something for you along the way with all the rejections, you better go be a dentist or change your profession," he says.

Fisher began his singing career as a cantor at The Great Synagogue of Tel Aviv in 1973 at the age of twenty-two. Through what he sees as the hand of God leading his life, he has gone on to perform on Broadway, in sold-out concerts around the world and in his own one-man shows. He also has recorded twenty CDs and dubbed and sang the voice of Moses in the Hebrew version of the animated feature film *The Prince of Egypt.* Throughout his journey, he has waited for God to show him the next step. "The puzzle of my life is that no human being could have put this together. It had to be a heavenly hand."

Unlike other actors whose biggest challenge may be to prove they are good enough for a part, Fisher has had to do that along with finding a producer willing to excuse him from performing on Friday nights and Saturday afternoons. As an Orthodox Jew who observes the sabbath, Fisher has had a career path "a hundred times more difficult than any actor or singer. My career would have been a hundred miles ahead of where it is now."

But for him, the career he has is the one God has provided, with the acting part an unexpected twist. It came about in 1986 while he was in London to sing in a concert of cantorial music for a children's charity. Since he had relatives in the city, he told the concert producer he would stay with his family so the charity could save the cost of his hotel accommodations. That thoughtful gesture changed his life.

While visiting with his cousin she mentioned she had seen a new musical recently and pictured him in the lead. He had never heard of the show, *Les Misérables*, and wasn't interested in seeing it. His cousin prevailed, and when he saw Colm Wilkinson, London's original Jean Valjean—the hero with an extraordinary love for God—he was transfixed. "I said: 'I can sing this. I can do this. I have to do this.'" It didn't matter that he had never acted and the part he wanted was the lead in a major musical. "From one moment to the next my confidence became so much bigger. By the time it ended I was Jean Valjean."

Having identified a role he wanted, he then had to go about securing it. He found out *Aluvei Ha'Haim*, the Hebrew-language version of *Les Misérables*, was coming to Israel, so he asked his manager to get him an audition. But the producers didn't share his enthusiasm. They had never heard of the cantor from Tel Aviv. Besides, they had their hearts set on a big name. Fisher persisted and got an audition. He was No. 18, and as he waited he listened to the other performers, who mostly sang Hebrew songs. Fisher had memorized all the show's songs in English and when his time came he sang "Bring Him Home," a prayerful song Valjean sings asking God to keep his future son-in-law safe while fighting with the revolutionaries in 1832 Paris.

After Fisher stopped singing, the producers stopped auditioning. No. 19 and all the others after didn't have a chance. The producers realized they didn't need a big name after all.

But the happily-ever-after part doesn't start there. After the producers told Fisher they wanted him, he told them about the catch—he would not perform on the sabbath or Jewish holidays. This shouldn't have been a problem in Israel, but since some rehearsals were held on the weekends and the production was scheduled to go on the road, where kosher restaurants would not always be available, the producers thought they would have to restart the audition process.

Then God, in the person of London producer Cameron Mackintosh, stepped in. He told the producers if they didn't use Fisher he would take him to London for that production. And so they said yes, and Dudu Fisher began his acting career by spending the next three and a half years as Jean Valjean in Israel. He would, in time, perform the role in London's West End and on Broadway, where he became the first actor in a starring role to be excused from performing for religious reasons. "For me to find Cameron Mackintosh and Richard Alexander (Mackintosh's assistant), they were two people sent to me by God."

Despite the fact that this cantor had never acted, Mackintosh, after seeing Fisher as Valjean in Israel, asked him to assume the role on Broadway, even though this meant hiring another actor to perform the role on Friday nights and Saturday matinees—at full pay since that actor would not be able to take another show. "It was like a real miracle. I can't put it in any other words," says Fisher who asked Mackintosh why he was willing to make such a financial investment in him. "What kind of producer would do such a thing?" Mackintosh said the production in Israel was the best he had seen, telling Fisher when he sang "Bring Him Home," he "felt the audience and the whole building were electrified."

Fisher explained that in Israel every person has or has had a family member in the army; he himself has two children serving. "In Israel when you sing 'Bring Him Home,' it means something." It meant something to Fisher each time he sang it for more than a thousand performances. He considers *Les Misérables* the best show written in the twentieth century, "no doubt about it," even better "than all the operas written in the twentieth century. What caught me was the music. Every song is powerful. I felt like it was written for me. Also the character of this person. I felt I don't have to play him—I am him. I live it, every step of my life praying and looking for God."

The thought of playing Valjean in New York made Fisher a little apprehensive before he arrived, not because he doubted his performing skills but because he was unsure how his fellow actors would react to his only doing six shows a week while they did eight. When he arrived at the theatre, however, he realized he need not be concerned. Someone had put a sign on his dressing room door that read: "Dudu Fisher: Jean Valjean. Friday night and Saturday matinee: Shabbos Goy." (A *shabbos goy* is a non-Jew who performs a task for an observant Jew on the sabbath.) In addition to keeping the sabbath on Broadway, he wore a *tallit*, a religious prayer shawl, and kissed the *mezuzah*, a container holding the *Shema* prayer, "Listen, O Israel: Adonai is our God, Adonai alone," hanging on his dressing room door before each performance. During Hanukkah he lit menorah candles backstage and served latkes to the whole cast.

Before seeing *Les Misérables* for the first time, Fisher had never heard of Victor Hugo, the author of the book on which the musical is based. "I was in Yeshiva schools," he says, laughing. "We just learned the Talmud and the Bible." And even though Jean Valjean is often seen as a Christ-figure created by the nineteenth-century Roman Catholic author, for Fisher the character's faith makes him universal. "The God of the Muslims, Christians, and Jews is the same God. There's no difference between Gods."

It is to that God Fisher prays before each performance. As the curtain goes up and he sees all the people in the audience, he thanks God for his talent and asks that everything—including the lighting and sound—will go right.

This faith has been central to Fisher all his life. It was necessary, he says, growing up in Israel in the 1950s. The country was filled with

Holocaust survivors and people with severe psychological problems. His grandfather, who left Lithuania at thirty-two, lost the eleven brothers and sisters he left behind. His father was saved by a non-Jewish family that hid him in Poland. "You had to believe there was a hand that saw you and was going to care for this world. There's always the question of why did this have to happen, but you can't have answers for everything. You give answers to the good things and always say the good things are seen from above."

To sustain this faith, Fisher says set prayers morning and night—"in between the lines there are always personal prayers"—keeps kosher, observes the sabbath, and goes to synagogue. "I live my life with my family in the Orthodox Jewish way."

Part of this religious Jewish experience actually helped make him an actor, he says, comparing being a cantor to being an actor. "A cantor, like an actor, talks about sadness, happiness, redemption, purity. The cantor stands with his back to the people and has to bring in all the people without arrangement or orchestra. They don't see your face, but you have to make them cry, be joyous, and dance in the aisles. You have to know how to act only with your voice." He no longer performs as a cantor in Israel but has been filling that role for more than two decades at Kutscher's Country Club in the Catskills for the High Holy Days and Passover.

Although Fisher leads a life based on faith in God, he says he doesn't try to convert others, although he has received indications he does have an influence. After singing to a sold-out crowd of 1,800 in Los Angeles in June of 2001, he received a letter from the show's manager. It mentioned the four encores and half a dozen standing ovations and said people had been "deeply inspired not just by his golden voice, but by his commitment and love for Judaism and Israel." It went on to say: "Never before have we received such unanimous accolades as we did over the Dudu Fisher concert. In addition, many have given strong consideration to start keeping shabbos because of Dudu's personal story."

Fisher's story is rooted in a belief that God will give him what he needs when he needs it. He keeps in mind the story of Abraham who had been told by God to sacrifice his son Isaac as a burnt offering to him. When Isaac saw they were approaching the altar, he asked his father where was the lamb to be sacrificed. Abraham's reply was that God will provide. And God, upon seeing Abraham's faith, provided a ram so that Abraham could spare his son. So Fisher sacrifices jobs to keep the sabbath, trusting God to provide others.

One way he has found to work in show business and still observe the sabbath is to do one-man shows. *Never on Friday* came out of his experience and has played in New York and around the United States. He calls it the cabaret story of his life and it always includes some jokes about his name—Dudu is a common nickname for David in Israel, but in America it's always good for a laugh. His most recent show, *Something Old, Something New*, played Off-Broadway in the fall of 2002.

These shows are especially challenging, since Fisher alone has to hold the audience, and he has been advised to reserve some energy and not use it all each night. This advice he doesn't follow, believing he should give whatever he has inside at each performance. "Tomorrow, please God, will be another day," is the way he thinks of it.

Fisher uses scripture commentary by Jewish sages to explain why his work is important in Judaism—if you can "make people to show their teeth—*tov le'ven shinayim me"halav*"—you have done the best thing you can do. "If you put a smile on somebody's face, you earn eternal life. If you make them feel good for a couple of hours, maybe more if they still talk about the show or feel good about it, you have done the greatest thing a person can do."

Growing up Baptist in Cleveland is a far different experience from growing up Orthodox Jewish in Tel Aviv. But like Fisher, Michael

McElroy, an actor and founder/director of the gospel choir Broadway Inspirational Voices, believes strongly that God has a plan for his life. And, like Fisher, he was raised in a family where religion was important. "I grew up with church as the center of my life," he says, explaining that his grandfather was a minister at the Harvest Missionary Baptist Church, as was his stepfather later. His grandmother played the piano and directed the choir, in which he sang with his mother, brother, sister, aunt, and uncle. "Our family was the heart and center of that church and also the musical center." His experience of singing in the choir stayed with him, prompting him to start a gospel choir of theatre people once he hit New York years later. "I had a strong sense of music, especially gospel music."

Church and gospel music were two early influences. The third element in the life of this future Broadway performer was musical theatre, which his uncle, a music director, and his mother, a theatre lover, exposed him to early. "Anything that came through town we saw. From a young age I loved theatre."

That love of theatre landed him in New York in 1990 after graduating with a BFA in drama from Carnegie Mellon University. His faith sustained him through show closings and going in and out of productions. "I was brought up in the church and in my family to have faith and hope and a connection to God. I believe there's a course and direction for my life. That takes a lot of pressure off. If I've wanted a job and didn't get it, I believe everything will happen when it's supposed to happen."

It would seem a career in show business is exactly the course God had in mind for McElroy. He got an agent shortly after arriving in the Apple and his first job, in the ensemble of *Richard III*, a New York Shakespeare Festival production starring Denzel Washington. When that closed, he tried the job most actors take on at some point—waiter. He admits he was pretty awful at it, but evidently it wasn't part of his plan. After one month he was offered the national tour of *Sarafina!* He never waited on another table.

His path in the theatre world continued when he got a part in *Miss Saigon* on Broadway, just one year after arriving in New York. That was followed by *The Who's Tommy* on Broadway. But after thirteen months in *Tommy*, McElroy began questioning this path. He wanted more than singing and dancing in the chorus, so when Jeanine Tesori, *Tommy's* assistant director, asked him to take the part of Flick in a workshop of *Violet*, a new musical, he left the steady income of a Broadway show with nothing on the horizon except the nominal pay for a workshop piece that would possibly never develop into a staged production. Once again it seemed he was following the right path. "That role changed the course and direction of my career. It catapulted me into a different place." And he never went back to the chorus.

Violet, based on the short story "The Ugliest Pilgrim" by Doris Betts, did have a staging, at Playwrights Horizon, a well-respected Off-Broadway theatre company, and McElroy's performance earned him a Drama Desk Award nomination. But when the show failed to move to Broadway, McElroy was devastated. "It was my first lesson of this business. Sometimes things are really good, but that doesn't matter. It's what sells, or what the people in power think will sell."

McElroy returned to Broadway in *Rent*, which meant being in a successful show and not having to audition again for a while. He stayed for more than two years before going into a new Broadway musical, *The Wild Party*, which failed to please critics or attract audiences and closed after sixty-eight regular performances. McElroy went back to *Rent* for seven months and then felt it was time to take another look at his path. "I was burnt out. I didn't want to do theatre anymore. I wanted to go back to music."

Despite feeling ready for a change, he decided to stay on the theatre path after he was asked to audition for the lead in *Blue*, a new musical going into production Off-Broadway by the Roundabout Theatre Company. He got the part, starring opposite Phylicia Rashad of *The Cosby Show* fame, playing a man in his fifties, which aged him a couple of decades. Although he recorded the show's CD, *Blue* failed to move to Broadway. But his performance opened two new doors. He was offered the part of Jaguar Dupree in *Thunder Knocking on the Door*, a blues musical headed for Trinity Repertory Company in Providence, Rhode Island, for which he wouldn't even have to audition. When the show moved to Off-Broadway months later, McElroy went with it.

Being offered a role without auditioning was a first for him, as was a following offer—the chance to record his gospel choir. It came about after Tom Jung attended Broadway Inspirational Voices' fall 2001 concert. Jung had been wanting to record a gospel choir for his small record label, dmp, and he approached McElroy. "Everything happens when it's supposed to," McElroy says. "It was something we were prepared for." McElroy was given total creative control and *Grace* was recorded in four days after four rehearsals. What took some time was choosing the title. " 'Grace' is such a simple word, but it says so much. It's the amazing grace God gives you that steps in and allows you to blossom. God's grace allowed us to do this."

And it allows McElroy to keep going.

"I try to learn with every experience. Then when the next opportunity comes along, I'm prepared. I try to grow as a person, to be the best I can be, so I can be in a constant state of being prepared."

Steady faith doesn't mean he is without doubts, though. He was concerned about going into a hit show like *Rent* as a replacement actor and he wondered if he could pull off becoming middle-aged for *Blue*. But he sees those doubts as a prod to move him along the path. "Every time something scares me, I know I should do it."

McElroy doesn't think God has singled him out because he's special. Rather he feels that being open to God allows him to see the blessings. "I believe God has really touched my life. When things are not happening the way I want them to, I don't lose hope. It's all part of preparing me for the next thing, without losing that sense of being open and vulnerable."

Tony Award–winning actor Kristin Chenoweth also believes God is guiding her life. She was raised a Southern Baptist in Broken Arrow, Oklahoma, a suburb of Tulsa, with a strong belief in God. And she relies on that belief now, living as she does in a world of uncertainty, where Broadway shows close quickly and a TV series ends weeks after it begins, both of which she has experienced.

"Faith is something a lot of people relate to as a God-thing, but it's also faith in yourself," Chenoweth says. "I've met a lot of actors who have faith in themselves. You either have faith or you don't. I choose to have faith. I believe it's a choice."

And for her, faith is a God-thing.

"He is with me like an old friend who's always present. If I feel distant from God it's because I've moved away."

Chenoweth's faith stems from her childhood, growing up in a devout Christian household and attending services Sunday morning and evening, as well as Wednesday evening at the First Baptist Church of Broken Arrow. She felt the call to commit herself to her faith early, becoming a Christian at Vacation Bible School when she was nine. Hers was a conservative Christian world, with members of her church going door-to-door "witnessing" to share their faith. Although Chenoweth never felt inclined to join them, and she's even less inclined to go door-to-door sharing her faith in Manhattan, she does give witness in ways appropriate for her life.

"I think the best way to do it is to try to live the best way you can so people will see something in you and will ask you. That gives you a perfect opportunity to tell them what you believe. I'm wary of beating people over the head. I love it when people say, 'Why are you happy?' It's more inviting when people want to know."

She speaks about her faith when asked and will even bring up the subject with interviewers who rarely, if ever, address subjects of a spiritual nature. "As a performer, you try hard to keep your views private, but it's a part of who you are, the spiritual side. It's such a big part of who I am."

Another way she has of quietly witnessing is wearing a small diamond cross, bought with money she made from the ABC movie version of *Annie*, in which she played Lily St. Regis. "It was the first big gift I bought for myself ever." She spotted it in a store after lunching with Kathy Bates one day and "obsessed about it forever." When Bates later asked if she had bought the cross, Chenoweth said no. Bates asked again another time and when Chenoweth still said no, Bates replied: "If you don't buy it, I'll buy it for you." Chenoweth bought the cross and now wears it everywhere she goes.

As for nurturing her faith, she ponders the day's scripture selection from the devotional *Our Daily Bread*, reads Psalms and Proverbs, and attends Sunday services at St. Paul & St. Andrew Methodist Church on the Upper West Side of Manhattan, which she likes because it's accepting of different people. When she's in California, she worships at the nondenominational Grace Church in Malibu, which she calls awesome. "It's closer to the way I was raised. They have a great contemporary band."

But she doesn't need to be in church to feel God's presence. "I see evidence of God every day. I feel led in my career. I haven't been in a Broadway hit, but He's blessed me with being able to do a lot of different roles. That's a gift."

Her strong belief in God affects her reactions to the ups and downs of life—and she's had her share of both. One night she won a Tony Award as best featured actress in the revival of *You're a Good Man, Charlie Brown*; the next morning the show, which was struggling to find an audience, posted a closing notice. She was given her own TV series on NBC, but *Kristin* was canceled after five episodes in the summer of 2001.

"I don't want to sound like a Pollyanna, but I have a tendency to look at the positive. That comes from the peace of knowing God in

Jesus Christ. I'm really about Jesus Christ and him being sent to save us from our sins."

Chenoweth still turns to her parents with questions about life and faith. She calls her mom an "awesome Christian lady" and her dad a wise man and says both are nonjudgmental about people of other faiths and ways of life. That's important to her now that working in show business and living in New York have altered her thoughts on homosexuality and people of different religions.

"Where I grew up it was all church. I didn't see a temple or a Muslim until I moved to New York. I grew up in the Bible Belt, but I have to differ in belief from the people I grew up with."

Her perspective began to widen even before she moved to New York, first as an undergraduate at Oklahoma City University, where she stayed to complete a master's in opera performance. But her views really shifted when she landed in New York and began dating men of different faiths. "I realize it's not just my belief out there. I have been enriched by a lot of people."

And she hopes she enriches others. "If I died tomorrow, I want people to say, 'She was a good example. She lived what she believed.'"

Larry Collis shares a similar background to Chenoweth's: he grew up Methodist in Lohrville, Iowa—population about 1,000—and shares her faith that show business is the right career. But he differs greatly in one thing: it took him a while to see God leading him to an acting career. Collis spent nearly two decades as a corporate banker before deciding he loved his avocation—performing in musical theatre—far more than his vocation, which he considered empty and unfulfilling. But choosing to pursue acting cost him his first marriage.

"When you decide to do something like this, there is definitely faith involved," he says. "For a lot of the time at first you feel inadequate, but the more you do it the more confident you become. It all boils down to faith in yourself."

That faith in himself has led him from Lohrville to Manhattan and roles on and off Broadway, as well as in films, soaps, and commercials. He realizes he took the wrong path initially in the 1950s when his father told him to major in engineering. "It was the dumbest thing I have ever done. I could hardly wait to get through school to get to band practice. You've got to listen to that voice no matter what the expense."

And once someone makes that faith decision, whether it's as a young person or later in life, it needs to be done without questioning. "You have to shut the door behind you. If you don't fully commit, it's not going to work."

In Judaism, fully committing means taking action, since it is not a creedal religion like Christianity, says Rabbi Richard Steinberg, senior rabbi of Congregation Shir Ha-Ma' A Lot in Irvine, California. "Judaism defines itself by what we do instead of what we believe. That's not to say faith isn't important. Belief is very important—it just doesn't happen to be the primary factor. How you act defines you as a Jew."

For Jews, this means wrestling with all the different ideas of what it means to be Jewish, Steinberg says, mentioning an old joke about two Jews and three opinions. The primary guide in this challenge is the *mitzvah*, or the divine commandments. "You could be as angry as heck with God, but you still have to obey the commandments." Acting on those commandments has always come first, Steinberg says, explaining that in the Book of Exodus when Moses presented the commandments to the people, they responded that they would do them, then understand them. "The word *Israel* means one who wrestles with God, not one who believes in or has faith in

God. God tells Jacob you have struggled with beings divine and human and have prevailed."

Steinberg says that while Jews don't have a creed the way Christians do, many are guided by the Thirteen Principles of Maimonides, a medieval doctor and philosopher. His articles of faith are: (1) the existence of God, which is perfect and sufficient unto itself and which is the cause of the existence of all other beings; (2) God's unity, which is unlike all other kinds of unity; (3) the prohibition against conceiving of God in bodily terms, and the understanding that anthropomorphic expressions applied to God in scripture are metaphorical; (4) the eternal nature of God; (5) the belief that God alone is to be worshiped and obeyed—there are no mediating powers able to freely grant man's petitions, and intermediaries must not be invoked; (6) prophecy; (7) the primacy of Moses as a prophet; (8) the belief that the entire Torah was given to Moses; (9) the belief that Moses' Torah will not be abrogated or superseded by another divine law nor will anything be added to, or taken away from, it; (10) the omniscience of God; (11) the belief that God rewards those who fulfill the commandments of the Torah and punishes those who transgress them; (12) the coming of the Messiah; and (13) the resurrection of the dead.

The challenge is to understand what God is saying, Steinberg says. "It can be frustrating because Judaism is more about process and questions than final destination. I define faith as belief in something for which you have no proof, and that's not easy for Jews. Jews are hands-on people. We like to see it, touch it, know it. I think that's why Jews gravitate to the arts and acting and comedy. It's a way of searching out the true meaning of life and what it has to offer. If I act like somebody else I might find the truth."

Looking for the truth led Steinberg to the rabbinate. After graduating from California State University at Hayward with a degree in criminal justice, he worked as a community service officer and became involved with a number of Jewish organizations. He then started thinking about becoming a rabbi and, encouraged by the rabbis he consulted, entered Hebrew Union College–Jewish Institute of Religion. "It's not a call from God as in Christianity; it's a call from the community." He studied in Jerusalem his first year, returned for the next two to the Los Angeles campus, and spent his final two years at the Cincinnati campus.

While in Cincinnati, he attended the funeral of a police officer who had been murdered. The priest's sermon explained that what happened was meant to be and that the officer had gone to a better place. "As a Jew, it almost made me sick to my stomach because it made no sense. I could see how that could be comforting to the family and I was envious of their faith, but that's not Jewish faith, or at least not this Jew's. It ain't that easy."

Steinberg spoke of the challenge to understand such violent deaths in a sermon delivered to his congregation during the High Holy Days in 2001, two weeks after the terrorist attacks of September 11. "I struggle for answers to the questions that pull on my heart, and tonight I am left with only one thing, which is my faith." He told them two obvious answers are to say God doesn't exist and that the tragedies happened for a reason. "Both leave me empty and still searching for answers. . . . I am left with creating my own faith, my own belief system that resonates with who I am, and what I believe, and I would like to share with you tonight."

He explained that an Orthodox Jew's faith "is abundantly clear. The definition of an Orthodox Jew, at its very core, is all about acceptance, the faith, if you will, in the idea of *Torah mi Sinai,* Torah from Mt. Sinai. In other words, it happened as the Bible so states. God gave the Torah to Moses, who gave it to the people as it was revealed to him. Indeed, it takes great faith to believe that the Torah is literally true, word for word, and that we are obligated as Jews to follow its every mandate."

For Reform Jews, he preached, what one believes is not so defined. "Questions about faith are very personal, questions that can only be answered by each of us individually. . . . Judaism at its very core is about the personal journey. . . . I always laugh when I hear the expression a 'leap of faith' for it is redundant. Having faith is rather a leap of reason, of logic and of evidence."

As for the notion that the death of the officer and all the people in New York, Washington, and Pennsylvania was God's will, Steinberg said his faith rejects that. "For if I did believe that this young man's death or the murder of all those innocent victims was God calling them home, all I could think is, what a cruel God who would cause such an occurrence, who would allow such things to happen."

Then he shared with his congregation what he did have faith in, even without proof. "First, I believe that we are created in the divine image and that divine image gives each human being the possibility to achieve goodness in their lives. Second, I believe that everything in the world does not happen for a reason—in that I have great faith. And last, I believe in the coming of better time for this world, a messianic time if you will, even though all the evidence, all the proof, is to the contrary. . . . If I believed everything happened for a reason, I know that I could not believe in God. A God who causes bad things to happen to people, for whatever the reason, would be too cruel a God in which to believe. And so I have faith in just the opposite, that everything does not happen for a reason, that God has nothing to do with the terrible things that happen in our lives. I take great comfort in the idea that no one person is chosen because of his deeds or misdeeds. The randomness of nature works in a way that is indiscriminate when it comes to human beings."

It is people's response to the chance circumstances of life which can reflect God, he preached. "My God, the God in which I have faith, is limited to only goodness as reflected in the divine image we human beings bring to earth. . . . The cause of terrorism had nothing to do with God, but the response by the best of humanity had everything to do with God. . . . Our world is facing great challenges and uphill battles, but my point is, why try fixing it if you don't actually believe you can change it? I do believe we can change it. And the whole concept of actually believing that there will be no more war or hunger, no more homelessness or crime, no more evil or destruction in my mind is all dependent on my first article of faith—that we were created in the divine image."

Steinberg preached about the terrorist attacks not just because they were so much on people's minds at that time but also because the issues raised are ones with which Jews continually grapple. Judaism is psychologically sound in its theology of death and dying, he says, but its understanding of heaven and what happens after death is underdeveloped. "It's never easy to be Jewish. As Israel, we're always struggling with God." The one thing Jews can count on is the monotheism of the *Shema*, the prayer found in Deuteronomy that tells Israel that the Lord their God is one God. "If you're going to have faith, have it in that one idea."

And don't give up the struggle. "I'm constantly trying to develop my own theology to understand the role God plays in my life," says Steinberg, who teaches a course at his synagogue about how Jews and Judaism are portrayed in films and on TV. "I try to encourage people to develop their own Jewish theology. We still have to act, but it's a lot more meaningful if there's faith and reason behind it. The more we study, the more we understand our belief system and the more we can define it."

The Rev. Paul D. Schmiege, pastor of St. Luke's Lutheran Church in New York's theatre district, says that in nearly every religious tradition, faith is a word that represents confidence in life after death, which has no moral values, striking the good and the bad, the young and the old. Faith is part of our universal desire for the divine, "a word of life that means there's something more. That awareness is the central element of faith."

It also feeds the creative process. "This drive shows up in all our arts, that there is something beyond the power of death and it gives life to us. Drama is one of the most obvious places this is articulated. Characters struggle with a sense of the inevitability of death and a sense of punishment, which is articulated either comically or tragically. We leave the theatre with a basic sense of injustice or transcendent justice at the experience of someone else's life. That's faith. It's intangible, unobservable, but we believe it's true."

Schmiege says in the Lutheran tradition faith is seen as a gift and opposes the idea that one has to accumulate certain attitudes and behaviors to be closer to God. "The important thing is there isn't anything we have to do or can do. God announces he's come to be close to us. Faith is the discovery this is true."

This is liberating, Schmiege says. "We don't have to do anything to have a sense of the presence of God. It's active on the part of God and passive on the part of human beings." Where humans beings do act is in deciding how to respond. "It's gift theology. Do I open it and say 'thank you' or do I say 'I've got six of them already.' In genuine gift giving, nothing is done to get the gift. That would contradict the idea that it's a gift. Faith is constantly tied up with gift and reception."

Schmiege cites the example of the last person Jesus saved on earth, a thief who was crucified beside him. When the thief proclaimed from his cross his belief that Jesus was God, Jesus told him he would join him that day in paradise. "That's the undeservedness of faith. For good people this is awful stuff," Schmiege says, explaining that most people believe that if you are good you will be rewarded and if you are bad you will be punished. "The system doesn't work that way."

A belief in faith as an undeserved gift was part of Martin Luther's argument against the medieval church and scholastics who said faith was defined by knowledge, agreement, and trust, Schmiege says, adding that for Luther the true definition dealt only with trust. Contrary to the teachings of the Roman Catholic Church, he did not emphasize the equal importance of good works. "Luther was accused of abandoning the Christian way of life," Schmiege says. "Luther said,

'Yes, but when we receive a gift we are grateful. We can't wait to do what pleases the giver.'"

For Schmiege, cities like New York illustrate how faith is a gift. "It's in cities that Christianity could take off. God is present in an undeserved way and can touch anyone. Christianity in rural and suburban areas is static and moralistic, dependent on community structures." Schmiege can walk out his door and encounter a homeless man whose life may not be too far removed from his own; possibly just a bad break or trusting the wrong person separate them. "There's tremendous diversity, a huge interplay of ideas and awareness of different lifestyles mixing. Christianity leapt from city to city."

Schmiege has been back in Manhattan since taking over as St. Luke's pastor in 2000. Although he grew up in small towns in Minnesota, he fell in love with the city after moving to New York following his 1977 graduation from Harvard Divinity School, from which he holds a master of theology. He served as assistant pastor at Immanuel Church in Manhattan and, most recently, spent five years at St. Anne's Church on Gresham Street in central London. "My ministry grew up in the urban environment."

St. Luke's is definitely urban. It is in the heart of the performing arts community, on Forty-sixth Street's Restaurant Row, and the heart of Times Square, which has been greatly cleaned up in recent years but is still home to some who are poor and disenfranchised and others who are caught up in drugs and prostitution. St. Luke's ministers to both worlds with its own Off-Broadway theatre in the basement and outreach programs, including a soup kitchen, clothing distribution program, and aid to refugees and immigrants.

Theatre people without affiliation turn to this Tudor Gothic church for weddings, funerals, and AIDS memorials. Actor Gregory Hines danced down the aisle at one service; the cast of the Broadway show *Your Arms Too Short to Box with God* performed at another.

Although about a third of St. Luke's 150 members work in the performing arts, Schmiege says he doesn't cater his services to them.

"We try to be broader, not for any single career or mind-set." Still, he thinks that one-third may be more dependent on faith than the others. "There's an awareness of the element of spontaneity, of the sheer creative grace that's present. Actors are more open in part because faith is a creative action. It's a spark that comes from beyond us. Actors must learn their skills, but that has nothing to do with the spark that comes. People live their lives looking for that moment of spark."

While it may seem actors are more open to faith, it is potentially present in everyone, Schmiege says. "What we do is awaken awareness of it. This probably never happens through formal religion, although it could be through a religious person. More often it's in discovery, an event through which something transcendent enters into our lives. This is where music and art and drama all play a role." Standing in front of Monet's paintings of waterlilies or going to a Broadway musical can prompt this experience. "They awaken a sense of moving beyond one's self. It's what it does to our hearts."

He sees this easily in shows like *Thoroughly Modern Millie*, with the young woman's determination to make it in New York. "It's a musical dedicated to faith and that as an individual I matter." He sees it in *Morning's at Seven*, Paul Osborn's 1939 play about four aging sisters that asks the question: What's it all about? "That's a faith cry." And, of course, in *Les Misérables*, a play about "redemption and justice and life after death. Theatre opens us to a way we can safely be shaped. When we watch a play or a musical, it lifts us beyond ourselves and we have once again pushed the darkness back."

In the Moment

So teach us to number our days
that we may gain a wise heart.
~PSALM 90:12

I know that this very minute has history in it,
We're here.
~JERRY HERMAN, *Mame*

The practice of being present, or "in the moment" as actors say, has long-established roots in Eastern religions; in Zen the present moment is everything. It is also where we can best find God. As Abraham Joshua Heschel wrote in his 1951 book *Man Is Not Alone: A Philosophy of Religion*, "The art of awareness of God, the art of sensing His presence in our daily lives cannot be learned offhand. God's grace resounds in our lives like a staccato. Only by retaining the seemingly disconnected notes comes the ability to grasp the theme."

French philosopher and mystic Simone Weil defined her idea of being present when she said, "Absolute attention is prayer." Besides being a way to pray, practicing being in the moment is also calming, which is why it is emphasized in contemporary stress management courses. But long before anyone ever took a course to manage stress, Jesus was telling his followers how to do it: "Do not worry about tomorrow, for tomorrow will bring worries of its own. Today's trouble is enough for today."

Being in the moment has long been an aim of Catholic saints. In the eighteenth century, Brother Lawrence, a Carmelite monk, described it as the "practice of the presence of God." For him, God was to be found in every moment; even those spent scrubbing pots in the monastery kitchen could offer contemplative value. Chores are part of daily life, and Brother Lawrence knew we had to seek God there as well as in chapel because God is present in all aspects of our lives. In the following century, St. Elizabeth Ann Seton, founder of the Sisters of Charity, the first congregation of religious women in the country, told her spiritual daughters to "keep to what you believe to be the grace of the moment . . . do your best . . . and leave the rest to our dear God."

For twenty-first-century stage actors, keeping to the grace of the moment, or at least the discipline of staying focused, is vital because there are no retakes during a live performance. Doing a show eight times a week means saying the same lines over and over—sometimes twice in one day. Even with years of practice, it takes vigilance to stay present.

Actors also need to work on keeping their stage lives and their home lives separate, so they can be in the moment in each. That's Vanessa Williams's goal, one she works hard on as a mother of four, Broadway star, hit recording artist, actor in feature and TV films, and wife of L.A. Lakers basketball star Rick Fox.

"Being present is a gift you have when you're a child and you don't have a past or a future," she said during a dinner break at a restaurant across from the Broadhurst Theatre where she was appearing as The Witch in the Broadway revival of *Into the Woods*. "Then society gets to you and anxiety and remorse creep into your life and they don't allow you to be present." So she concentrates on remaining in the moment. "I try to incorporate it every day, to not remind myself of past failures and learn how to forgive and trust the future. It makes life easier to be in the present; it's just hard to do."

The question she is asked most is how she balances motherhood and a career. "There is no balance. Right now I'm on Broadway feeding my creativity and professional goals, and my children, unfortunately, are missing out on having me there for the nighttime rituals of homework and storytelling. But I'm performing before 1,200 people and this is what I feel called to do. When I'm not working, I can feel anxious about my professional life. There'll never be a balance, which is why we have to live in the moment. My kids know this is my passion and this is what makes Mom feel good. It's disappointing at times, but they accept it."

Part of Williams's being-in-the-moment experience of Broadway includes greeting the large number of fans who wait for her outside the stage door, even though she still has an hour's commute to her home in Westchester County. She spends as much as twenty minutes signing autographs and posing for pictures.

But when she shifts focus, she enters completely into a different moment. She took a break from *Into the Woods* to fly to Maine to see her daughter dance in a summer camp production. "Then I'm into Mom mode again to make up for not being at parents' weekend and not being at visiting day because I'm on Broadway." After the trip to camp, even though she hadn't had a break for herself in many months, she headed back to New York and right into a two-show day. "That's the balancing act I try to do."

But even back on Broadway, it takes effort to stay present. "I can be singing and going over my grocery list in my mind. My mouth can be disconnected from my brain because I'm on automatic pilot until I catch myself and snap out of it because I haven't been in the moment. That's the danger of doing eight shows a week. Then there are nights when I feel excited and challenged and am on. That's the key, to try to make it new each night."

That's also the key for Casey Groves when he prepares to take on the role of Father Damien, which has become a calling for Groves, who first assumed the part of the Belgian-born priest in Aldyth Morris's one-man play, *Damien*, as a sixteen-year-old at De La Salle High School in New Orleans. In the years that followed, Groves studied acting at the College of Santa Fe, the Royal Academy of Dramatic Arts, and the British American Drama Academy and earned a master's in spirituality at Holy Names College in Oakland, California. Then, more than a decade after that high school performance, he began thinking about Father Damien, who, with what Groves describes as his "everyday compassion," ministered to the lepers of Móloka'i, Hawaii, until his death from leprosy in 1889. The call to take on the character again as an adult was so strong Groves decided to revisit the role Off-Broadway in 2000.

During the performances, he forgot one of the primary elements of acting and of the spiritual life—the importance of being in the moment. "There were times during the hour-long performance that I would wonder if the audience was getting bored and it made me self-conscious." So before a performance the following year at the Passionist monastery in Queens, New York, Groves studied Father Damien's picture intensely during the subway ride to the community. As he rehearsed in the space, he pictured Father Damien moving through the room.

It worked.

"I lost my self-consciousness. I let Father Damien speak. His image was with me the whole time. I was so immersed in his world that it was like I could feel my face becoming like his, with his intensity. I could feel the muscles in my face dropping into place."

One element of the priest's face in particular struck Groves. "His eyes had the same look, a real intensity when he was young and twenty years later when he was full of leprosy and his ear was falling off." Groves keeps that image of Father Damien's eyes when he goes onstage. "I transfer my heart center to my eyes. You have to be present to do it."

To develop his ability to be present, Groves studies Zen meditation two or three days a week, and sometimes all day Saturday, with the Rev. Robert E. Kennedy, S.J., at St. Peter's College in Jersey City, New Jersey. "In acting, there's a lot of being present to images. It's Tibetan in that way. You have to create the images. I have to see the lepers' faces, their wounds, and their ulcers, to see the island, the house where Father Damien lived and the tree he slept under the first night, or else I'm not inhabiting that world and I'm not doing my job."

Besides Kennedy, Groves credits Tim Phillips, his acting teacher, with helping him stay in the moment onstage, as well as in preparing for an audition. One method Groves particularly likes is what Phillips calls "Sherlock Holmesing" a script. This is helpful for actors going into an audition cold, being handed a script they know nothing about and asked to read. "Most actors feel a little psychotic," Groves says. "You don't know where you are, who you are, you don't know anything about the character. That's why we feel so awkward in auditions."

In using the Sherlock Holmesing method, the actor starts with the script, let's say *Fool for Love* by Sam Shepard. Since the actor doesn't have time to read it, he looks for clues starting with the title, word for word. Groves says "Fool" makes him think of the Fool in *King Lear* and "Love" makes him think of Valentine's Day. The playwright's first name sounds Western to him and his last name makes Groves think of Christ and flock. Then, if the actor knows anything about the playwright's themes in other plays, she or he can consider those. A final consideration could be that character's name. In *Fool for Love* the name

May suggests to Groves spring and Guiniver. All of this helps the actor develop an instinct about the part that, when right, makes for a good audition. "By Sherlock Holmesing it you're looking for the universe in a grain of sand. It makes the whole process more playful, instead of just trying to impress someone. It's so much more creative, and as you do it more things start popping up. Because you're doing intuitive work the super-objective of the character arrives."

That's an effective technique for being in the moment of the audition. Groves also uses a Phillips technique for staying in the moment once he has a part. This involves discovering the character's relationship to persons, places, things and events. Groves worked with Phillips on this in preparation for an Off-Broadway run of *Damien* at the Jose Quintero Theatre in February 2002. The play begins in 1936 as Father Damien's body is being exhumed in Moloka'i to be reburied in a place of honor in Belgium. As Father Damien looks on, he is upset that he is being taken away from the people for whom he cared and died. The story follows his life backwards. As his casket passes Moloka'i on its ship journey, Father Damien recalls his arrival there and the years he spent ministering to the lepers and helping them build houses, gardens, roads, and docks. The play ends when the casket arrives back in his boyhood town and he happily looks upon his family's farmhouse and the priests' residence where his father left him on his twentieth birthday.

Groves had always portrayed Father Damien's joy at seeing his hometown again, but he hadn't considered how much that love of home was central to the character. In an opening scene, when Father Damien tells of seeing a casket arrive for his remains, it is draped in the Belgian flag. Groves had recounted that as narrative, with no emotion. After working with Phillips to see relationships, he realized that Father Damien would have been filled with emotion upon seeing the flag of his beloved country, which he left as a young man. When Groves portrays Father Damien now, that emotion is there. "When you find the relationships it makes it more complex and the connections are there from beginning to end. They're like Tarzan ropes—you swing from relationship to relationship."

Groves says this technique helps him stay in the moment while onstage alone for an hour presenting Father Damien's story. If his mind wanders, he can bring himself back quickly because he knows Father Damien so thoroughly he can reconnect with the emotion of the moment. "The relationships key me right back in because I can feel them. I know how Father Damien feels, so it's intuitive knowledge. I know where I am because I know the relationship to that event."

It is essential for actors to continue to develop methods for staying in the moment, Groves says. "Your craft is a sacred circle where magic can happen. Producers can come and go, directors can come and go, but your craft is your craft and you have to protect it."

When actors fail to stay present to their part, they are not the only ones to lose concentration. If they don't stay in their character's world, the audience doesn't either.

"The audience can see through you if you're not in the moment," Kristin Chenoweth says. For her this means staying focused. If you're at rehearsal, be there, she says, not making mental lists of all the things you have to do later. When you're in the play, be in only the scene you're in. "You can't get ahead of yourself," she says, explaining that when she has been anticipating a line that got a laugh the night before, it bombs because she has gotten ahead of herself and hasn't done the proper buildup. "If you get ahead, the audience gets ahead. You do only that scene so you experience it for the first time, each time. That's the number one challenge."

Staying focused and trying not to get ahead also apply when Chenoweth is doing a concert. Even in that venue, where a singer is much more apt to acknowledge the audience than in a play, she tries not to be distracted if someone shifts or yawns. "You have to get back to what you're singing about," she says, adding that if she is distracted she might be singing a line that could have really affected someone, but the opportunity will be lost if she is not in the moment. "I make it relate to me and get them out of my mind."

This technique certainly seems to be working. Her October 2002 season opening concert of Lincoln Center's American Songbook series drew a rave review from Stephen Holden in the *New York Times*. He described how Chenoweth "sashayed onto the stage . . . looking like Botticelli's Venus. Wearing a spangled powder-blue gown slit to the hip, her blond hair cascading down her back, this diminutive Broadway singer from Broken Arrow, Okla., was every inch the modern screwball glamour girl." He wrote of her "chameleon musical personality," with her ability to shift between a sugary lilt and an operatic soprano. "Ms. Chenoweth is, of course, both peppy and sweet, funny and sexy . . . she oozed a high-powered, down-home star quality . . . She's also consistently sensitive to the nuances of song lyrics." The ultimate test of her in-the-momentness—and her amazing voice—during that concert was her performance of a "ferociously difficult aria from *Candide*," which won her a standing ovation.

An accolade like that doesn't come just for a well-developed voice. It comes to people like Chenoweth who have learned not to get ahead of a line or a lyric and not to be distracted. She offers the advice of a college teacher, Vicki Kelly, who told students "do what you're doing while you're doing it." All people, not just actors, lose if they are not in the moment, Chenoweth says. "You miss a lot of blessings if you get ahead."

Being in the moment is essential offstage as well as on, as Richard Costa has learned. After appearing in the 1995 Broadway revival of *Gentlemen Prefer Blondes*, racking up credits which included the national tour of *Annie Get Your Gun* with Cathy Rigby, and the Radio City Spectacular, he faced years of rejections, so many rejections that he considered giving up on show business. Then, in 1998, he was cast in the roles of Hans and Rudy in the Broadway revival of *Cabaret*. The show was a hit, meaning that instead of struggling to keep his center through the rough cycle of auditioning and rejection, he had to learn to maintain that center playing the same parts eight times a week for many years.

"As an actor, you're always looking for the next job and thinking about the future," he says. "I'm in a long-running show, but it can be hard to relax and enjoy the moment. The steady income means I can play and have a life and get some savings behind me, but I want to be creative and always look for the next thing. I'm struggling to count my blessings and to enjoy now."

Besides a steady job on Broadway, Costa counts a great relationship as one of his blessings. The problem is that the two blessings are often at odds. His partner works all week during the day and has weekends off. Costa works nights and weekends, leaving them little time together. Even though Sunday mornings are one time they're both free, Costa has found sacrificing that time to sing in the choir at St. Malachy's/The Actors' Chapel helps him keep his center. "I'm thankful. That's not the issue, but everybody's experiences are relative. It's hard to talk to people who don't have long-running shows. I don't want to complain. That's why I come to St. Malachy's to be in the choir. It helps you to focus on other things than yourself, to reflect on what you have. You can be yourself here. It's not an audition and you're not being judged."

He does two shows on Saturday, getting to bed between 12:30 and 1:00 A.M. But the next morning he's at St. Malachy's by 10:00 to sing for the 11:00 Mass, later going to the theatre for two more shows. "I need it, to escape and reevaluate what I have. I wouldn't do it if I didn't love it so much and see the benefits outweighing the negatives."

Among the benefits he carries away is the ability to focus. "There are so many rejections—'You don't look right,' 'You're too tall'—you can feel you're not good. I have to home in on the fact that I am good. That's what got me here. It's a hard thing to learn, to let everything else go away and not second-guess yourself. I can find myself editing myself during an audition and that's wrong. You've got to go in and be yourself. If that's what the part calls for, it will open doors. Once you let your doubts go, the creative juices flow."

And when the rejections do come, especially the ones after several callbacks that are the most painful, Costa has learned how to stay in the moment of his life. "I go back to church and say 'thank you for the opportunity and help me not to ponder this and doubt myself.' Without a spiritual life I'd be so scattered I wouldn't know where to go. I need a sanctuary where it's calm. Church is familiar, it's in my background. It's a great place to go mediate, to go within myself."

In Judaism, being in the moment in prayer is achieved in *kavvanah*, or praying with intention, says Rabbi David Woznica, executive vice president for Jewish Affairs for the Jewish Federation of Greater Los Angeles and co-rabbi of the Synagogue for the Performing Arts in L.A. "It's praying and feeling the presence of God. It's hard to live in the moment every moment, but when it happens it's an amazing gift."

Being in the moment means not only feeling God's presence, but also focusing on an issue or the person one is with, "not having an ego or wondering what people are thinking," Woznica says. "It's trying to create holy or sacred moments."

Judaism helps in this. His friend Dennis Prager teaches that "the deed shapes the heart more than the heart shapes the deed," meaning that we should pray even when we don't want to because the act can lead into a connection with God. Woznica says the Hebrew verb for prayer, *l'heetpalel,* means to examine oneself. "Does God need to hear from David Woznica every morning? I'm not sure I think so, but I do think Woznica needs to reflect every morning. We will miss these moments when we feel God's presence if we don't pray because we don't feel like it."

As a rabbi, he is especially aware of the need to be in the moment. One minute he may be meeting with a couple about to be married and sharing with them their joy; then in a short time someone with a terminal illness can turn to him. "At that moment you need to have the ability to be there for them, to take everything else out of your mind and connect empathetically, to genuinely listen. That's the practice of being in the moment."

Woznica has practiced in a variety of ways. Before joining the Jewish Federation in Los Angeles, he was director of the Ninety-second Street Y's Bronfman Center for Jewish Life in Manhattan, one of the premier Jewish educational and cultural institutions in the United States. In his current position he is responsible for shaping the Federation's Jewish mission and vision for the new century. He also serves as a spiritual leader for the Synagogue for the Performing Arts, a nonaffiliated synagogue with close to five hundred members. Founded in 1973 by people from the entertainment community in Los Angeles, it holds services the first Friday of every month. Woznica calls the services "conservativish" because they are essentially a mix of traditional Hebrew and English prayers and rituals, but with an added emphasis on the performing arts that allows the cantor to create a different theme each month; some have dealt with comedy, musical theatre and Yiddish songs of the past.

Because being in the moment takes practice, one should consider the blessing of every moment with family, friends, or one's profession, although Woznica knows this is hard. He remembers being stopped in traffic on the freeway heading home from giving a lecture in San Diego. When cars began inching along, he came up to a horrible accident. He said a prayer for the people involved, then resolved to slow his own driving. "A minute and a half later I was back to normal speed. It's hard to capture that feeling. It's fleeting." What we need to do, he says, is remember our times of joy or sadness to help bring and keep us into the moment with others.

Woznica gives an example of a practice he learned from his co-rabbi at Synagogue for the Performing Arts, Rabbi Joseph Telushkin. When he hears a siren, instead of being annoyed that it interrupted his phone conversation or television program, he says a prayer for the person in the ambulance or the police or firefighters on their way to a call. "That's being in the moment. You have to be prepared to shift from talking with your friend to saying a prayer, but imagine how you would feel if you were in an ambulance and you knew everyone within earshot was praying for you. That's how we create sacred, holy moments."

He had an even earlier lesson in creating these sacred moments as a first-year rabbinical student. When he and other students returned from conducting services for the High Holy Days, their professor, Rabbi Marshall Meyer, asked them about their experiences. The consensus was the services had gone great and the students thought they would make wonderful rabbis. Then Meyer asked: "And did you pray?" Woznica, for one, was stunned. "I remember getting chills." He saw how easy it was to get caught up in the performance and lose sight of the reason for the service—to pray. "The whole issue of being a rabbi is to be in the moment and not thinking just about the congregation. If you're not praying, you're in a sense not being true to the call."

The rabbi is able to pray while leading a service because everyone in the service is praying together. "You're both a prayer leader and a member of the congregation at the same time. You're praying with the same prayer book, reading from the same Torah, rejoicing at the same joy, and crying at the same sadness. You're aware there are a lot of people there and at the same time not aware. You're not worrying too much about what people are thinking; you're trying to be genuine."

For this reason, Woznica, who lectures widely throughout the country, brings only bulleted comments when giving an address rather than a written-out lecture. "That allows me to be in the moment. I can flow into a tangent. If a story comes to mind or a new idea, then I am right there. When the speaker is right there, you can tell."

Jesuit priest Robert Kennedy stays in the moment by practicing Zen. He is one of only a handful of Jesuits in the world to bear the title Roshi, which means venerable Zen teacher. He uses his training to help Casey Groves and other actors, as well as hundreds of people in retreats throughout the year, practice this Eastern way of being present.

"It's all we have, really. The past and future are in our imaginations and dreams. The present never comes or goes away. It's always here."

Kennedy was familiar with the notion in Catholic spirituality of what is referred to as the sacrament of the present moment. But his ability to practice it was greatly enhanced when he encountered Zen while working in Japan in the late 1950s and early 1960s. "The Jesuits got me into this. The Jesuits in Japan were doing Zen." As a Christian, he could appreciate Zen as a gift to help him stay in the moment. "That's where God is found, where we expect to find reality. The way to make progress is to stay awake. I'm not trying to become a Buddhist. I am Irish, after all. I really needed a new way to be Catholic."

While God has revealed God's self through dreams, both in the Old and New Testaments, Kennedy says one has a better chance of finding God by staying aware in the present moment. "That's how we move the psyche forward, by staying conscious."

Allowing the mind to wander, especially in escapist ways like daydreaming, is "the way we have of comforting ourselves, like thumb-sucking," he says, adding that being present comes more naturally to some than others. "Romantics are never in the present moment. They're always in the past or future. People who are rooted in the senses find it easier."

Allowing the mind to obsess over things and repeat concerns over and over not only doesn't allow one to be in the moment but is exhausting as well. "That's why people are worn out and need vacations. The present moment should never exhaust us because it's never really the same."

One of the first fruits of practicing Zen is realizing how much our minds wander. "The mind is a drunk monkey. When you begin to practice Zen you realize how unfocused you are. Most of the day you're not conscious. People who don't try to control their minds don't realize how little control they have."

Controlling the mind, therefore, is as important for Christians as it is for Buddhists. "This moment God is completely manifest. God cannot be divided up. God is completely present in each moment." And in each of those moments God's will is revealed. Kennedy quotes Mother Teresa as saying she didn't know what God's plan for her was until she picked up her first leper and in caring for him found herself. He quotes St. Augustine: "I fear that Jesus will pass by and not come again."

Kennedy sees signs of in-the-momentness in Jesus. He was conscious of his father's will, yet was very much his own person. "It's hard to say anything in Nazareth made him that way," Kennedy says. He was observant of what was around him, which is evident in how he pointed out everyday things in making his case about worrying in his Sermon on the Mount. "Look at the birds of the air; they neither sow nor reap nor gather into barns, and yet your heavenly Father feeds them. Are you not of more value than they? And can any of you by worrying add a single hour to your span of life? And why do you worry about clothing? Consider the lilies of the field, how they grow; they neither toil nor spin, yet I tell you, even Solomon in all his glory was not clothed like one of these. But if God clothes the grass of the field, which is alive today and tomorrow is thrown into the oven, will he not much more clothe you—you of little faith? Therefore do not worry, saying, 'What will we eat?' or 'What will we drink?' or 'What will we wear?' For it is the Gentiles who strive for these things; and indeed your heavenly Father knows that you need all these things. But strive first for the kingdom of God and his righteousness, and all these things will be given to you as well."

Jesus also focused on the person he was with, Kennedy says. When he met a Samaritan woman at a well, he wasn't sidetracked when she questioned why he would talk to her, a person of lower standing and a woman. "He was a human being who seemed to understand people."

That focus is vital for Jesus' followers today when they receive the sacraments and participate in liturgy. "Any sacrament depends on our assent, and that depends on our consciousness. The church desperately needs something like Zen." He says Catholicism in practice has become something close to believing in magic, "the enemy of all true religion. People try to bend God through the sacraments. They try to get God to do what they want by bargaining with God. They perform the sacraments so God will do what they want. They're trying to buy God's favor. That's the magical element." He quotes President Abraham Lincoln who, when asked if God was on the side of the north, said he was interested only in whether the north was on the side of God. "In religion, we should try to resurrect ourselves to be on the side of God."

Kennedy helps others achieve presence at the Morning Star Zendo center he established in 1997 in Jersey City, New Jersey, at St. Peter's College, where he is a professor of theology and the Japanese language, and in retreats in the United States and Mexico. He also is the author of two books, *Zen Spirit, Christian Spirit: The Place of Zen in Christian Life* and *Zen Gifts to Christians*. Kennedy says he is not interested in converting anyone to Zen, but he cannot overemphasize the importance of practicing being in the moment. "Each moment is a new revelation, then the pathway closes. Others will open, but not that one. How could it? The moment never returns."

Listening

When the righteous cry for help, the Lord hears,
and rescues them from all their troubles.
~PSALM 34:17

Careful the things you say,
Children will listen.
Careful the things you do,
Children will see.
And learn.
Children may not obey,
But children will listen.
~STEPHEN SONDHEIM, *Into the Woods*

MANY OF THE answers for our lives are already inside us if we will just listen. Listening to others is important, of course, but when what they say doesn't feel right or contradicts what we're hearing within, listening to the inner voice, the source of one's creativity, is the smart choice. We have this on the highest authority. It can be found in the thirtieth chapter of the

Book of Deuteronomy, verses 11 through 14, in the words of the covenant the Lord commanded Moses to make with the Israelites: "Surely, this commandment that I am commanding you today is not too hard for you, nor is it too far away. It is not in heaven, that you should say, 'Who will go up to heaven for us, and get it for us so that we may hear it and observe it?' Neither is it beyond the sea, that you should say, 'Who will cross to the other side of the sea for us, and get it for us so that we may hear it and observe it?' No, the word is very near to you; it is in your mouth and in your heart for you to observe." Later the prophet Sirach reminds us: "If you are willing to listen, you will learn; if you give heed, you will be wise."

Attentive inner listening was also the answer for St. Benedict in fifth-century Rome. In the prologue of the rules he developed for his monks, he tells them: "Listen carefully, my child, to the master's instructions, and attend to them with the ear of your heart."

In the theatrical world, George Bernard Shaw gave us a character who knows how to listen like this in his play *St. Joan*. When Joan says she hears voices and they come from God, her friend tells her the voices come from her imagination. "Of course," she replies. "That is how the messages of God come to us."

For actors, once that inner voice, heard with "the ear of your heart," has been heeded and a role decided upon, then listening goes back to the standard person-to-person practice. Listening to what other actors onstage say before they speak keeps each performance fresh and helps create an appearance of honesty in the performance. It is important to listen to that night's dialogue and not just repeat lines that have already been said from memory many times.

Kristin Chenoweth works on both kinds of listening. She became a good actor by listening to her fellow performers onstage. But she became a Tony Award winner by listening to her inner voice. "If I'm quiet, I hear things in my heart, my spirit. When I listen, I have a sense of peace, of knowing."

She learned that from her parents who adopted her as an infant and with whom she holds a deep bond. "My parents always said to listen inside. It's kind of funny to say I'm adopted because I'm so much like my parents. They are the ones who helped me learn what that voice is inside. It's God. Sometimes I get so busy I can't hear it, but at least I recognize the problem. I need to get home and be with my family, and I need to be alone to listen."

The ability to listen that her parents helped her achieve also helped her discern her identity. While she always knew she was adopted, she has never had a desire to search for her birth parents because she feels she is the daughter of the parents who raised her.

She does wonder, coming from a nonmusical family, where her extraordinary voice comes from. And she says she may want to know about her biological parents for medical reasons when she is older or has a child of her own. But all her life she's been secure in her parents' love. "I am so fulfilled in my life and with my parents."

That gift they gave her of listening has proven to be crucial in her career. In 1999 when she was offered parts in two different Broadway revivals—Winnie in *Annie Get Your Gun*, starring Bernadette Peters, and Sally in *You're a Good Man, Charlie Brown*, everybody told her to take Winnie because the show was sure to have a long run. Sally was too risky, she was told again and again, because a revival of *Charlie Brown* could have trouble finding an audience.

She was lucky to have a month to make her decision, and she spent the time "talking to God" and listening to what God was saying rather than all the voices around her. "I prayed about it a lot and that peace came to me. The arrows were pointing to *Charlie Brown*."

As it turned out, what she heard from everybody else was right. *Annie Get Your Gun* ran for 1,045 regular performances; *Charlie Brown* closed after 149. But what she heard from God also was right. Ben Brantley, reviewing the show for the *New York Times*, called hers "one of those breakout performances that send careers skyward." And it did. A week before *Charlie Brown* closed, she won a Tony for best featured actress in a musical. And the next day ABC signed her to play Lily St. Regis in the TV movie version of *Annie*. Offers from casting directors, film studio directors, and Broadway producers followed. "That knowing, that peace wouldn't have come without listening," she says, calling listening "the vessel for God to speak to you."

"Sometimes I hear myself talk, saying I hear God talking in my heart, and I think if I weren't a Christian I'd think I'm a nut. All I know is it works for me. I can't imagine what I would have done if I had not known God."

When she again had to make a big career decision in 2001, she knew what to do—she went to God in prayer and listened. What she heard made her give up going to Broadway with a role she loved and had helped develop in workshop, that of Millie in *Thoroughly Modern Millie*, in favor of her own NBC series, *Kristin*. Sutton Foster, who took on the role after Chenoweth bowed out, went on to win a Tony Award in 2002 as Best Actress in a Musical, while *Kristin* ended up being canceled before the entire season aired. "It was a decision I had to make and it was hard and it continues to be hard because I look at the show and I love it." But she has no regrets. She had the honor of having her own show and she went on to play Marian in the ABC movie version of *The Music Man*, opposite Matthew Broderick as Professor Harold Hill. "I believe things happen for a reason. Sutton Foster is wonderful. As much work as I put into it, I believe it went to the right person, and I believe I was supposed to do *The Music Man*. It all worked out the way it was supposed to. I like to say I played a little part in creating the show. It was a great experience."

And she certainly wasn't through with Broadway. She planned to return in the fall of 2003 as Glinda, the Good Witch of the North, in *Wicked*, a new Stephen Schwartz musical based on the 1995 novel by Gregory Maguire.

This technique of listening within has been working for Chenoweth for some time. Listening to God made her give up her plan of becoming a contemporary Christian singer, which she had always assumed would be her future. After all, she had been singing since early childhood at the First Baptist Church of Broken Arrow, Oklahoma. "I grew up at church," she says. "That's where I gathered my skills and knowledge."

But during her five years at Oklahoma City University, from which she graduated with a master's in opera performance, she began to question some of her old ideas, and she continued questioning after moving to New York. She saw another future opening for her. Although she thinks it would have been easier to be a Christian singer, "this is where my path was."

It also would have been easier for her to be an opera singer since her voice was rapidly approaching a four-octave range. At twenty-two she earned the title of "most promising newcomer" at a Metropolitan Opera audition and was selected as one of five students to be given a scholarship to the Academy of Vocal Arts in Philadelphia for a four-year postgraduate program. But two weeks before she was to begin, she helped a friend move to New York and decided to audition for a role in *Animal Crackers*, a Marx Brothers musical, at the Paper Mill Playhouse in Millburn, New Jersey. When she got the part, she followed her inner voice to an acting career. Since then she's been in several Broadway shows, winning a Theatre World Award in 1997 for her part in *Steel Pier*, and has even been honored with that great showbiz endorsement, a celebrity caricature on the wall at Sardi's.

Writing about Chenoweth in *The New Yorker*, John Lahr said: "In an earlier time, when Broadway was a leader in popular culture and not a follower, Chenoweth's singing voice, her high-pitched speech (which sounds as if she had just inhaled helium), her comic timing, and her aura of downright decency would have made her one of America's sweethearts. . . . She's a God-fearing Baptist whose buoyancy is underpinned by the Bible's good news. Both her optimism and her talent are indicative of a more innocent era of entertainment."

But even in the struggles in this present era, she finds meaning. "I'm so happy for my upbringing, and I'm thankful God placed me in show business. I'm in a way a little soldier for Him in this business. I know I'm here for a reason."

In listening, she finds it.

Edward Herrmann also practices the art of listening. As an actor, he has been singled out for his mastery of this skill, but he strives to perfect it in his life as a convert to Catholicism as well. "There's a whole tradition in our beloved church of putting ourselves in the way of hearing God, be still and know." He sees this same process unfolding professionally. "As an acting technique, listening is very important. At first you want to act everything out. Later you learn to listen."

As an actor, Herrmann has had plenty of opportunity to develop this skill. After graduating from Bucknell University with a degree in drama, he headed to the Dallas Theater Center, where he spent three years. Paul Baker, DTC founder and former managing director, has described Herrmann as "always very intense and pleasant, with excellent manners" and "always in a good temper."

At twenty-five he won a Fulbright to study for a year at the London Academy of Music and Dramatic Art where he further developed his classical skills, worked on voice and diction, and learned stage fighting. "Classical training is good because it lasts and is always a service to your emotional life onstage," Herrmann has said.

That training has served him well on Broadway, where he earned a Tony Award for best featured actor in 1976 for his role in *Mrs. Warren's Profession* and nominations for his performances in *The Philadelphia Story* and *Plenty*. His films include *Reds*, *The Purple Rose of Cairo*, *The Cat's Meow* and *The Emperor's Club*. His most recent television role is that of

Richard Gilmore, the father and grandfather in the hit WB series *Gilmore Girls*, but he may be remembered best for his 1970s Emmy-nominated turns as FDR in the movies *Eleanor and Franklin* and *Eleanor and Franklin: The White House Years*.

Acting in any of these mediums, Herrmann says, always means listening to what someone tells you. "You don't react until you hear something you need to react to. In rehearsal you become more aware of waiting for something to happen. If you manufacture something you've worked on in your apartment, you may not connect with what can happen in rehearsal. It needs to be spontaneous, then something can happen. Your character bumps up against another character and is diverted, changed. The electrical current that's generated is the real experience. You can't do it unless you listen."

Listening is necessary even when a character has periods when he doesn't have to respond, as was the case in his 1983 Tony-nominated role in David Hare's *Plenty*. Nan Robertson, praising Herrmann's performance in a January 16, 1983, *New York Times* article, had this to say: "Edward Herrmann listens. He listens so intently, with his face and mind and body, that the audience is always aware of him. This is true for long moments when he does not have a single line to speak."

Herrmann has been listening intently on his faith journey as well as onstage. "In the spiritual life, it's the major discipline from the Zen masters to St. Thérèse," he says. It's a hard technique to develop, but when practiced it can lead to gratitude. "As actors we're all blessed or cursed with the need to show off. If you've had a good childhood or if you've had a bad childhood, you want to get up in front of other people and sing a song. You think it's something original, and it is original. It's also old—thanks for being here. If you're lucky enough to have the arts as your work, you become part of the spiritual life."

Which is why he imagines it must be harder for someone to work in business without a spiritual life. Because the spiritual element isn't so obviously present in the work, as important as that work may be, one could feel isolated. "I would venture to guess most people who work for companies or in trades don't think of their work as spiritual. That's why St. Thérèse values the humblest possible gesture as the will of the Father." As does Herrmann, which is why he took Benedict for his confirmation name, in honor of the saint credited with building up Western monastic spirituality and emphasizing the need to find God in work as well as prayer—and to listen with the ear of the heart.

Since finding God in work and prayer involves listening, Herrmann looks for ways to develop that ability. Focusing on something specific helps. "In Catholicism, concreteness can't be seen, but it can be felt. That's why you don't throw out the statues and the crucifix. They help focus us. The same technique is at work when you go to the movies and the logo of MGM or 20th Century-Fox comes on. It settles people. Now the audience is focused in one direction. We have to be careful, though, what we attach our concentration on."

And one should not be too attached to the symbols and miss the transcendence.

"What's the point of the arts as a discipline? It's absurd to pretend to be somebody else, a rabbit or Hamlet. It's silly, but it isn't. We don't begin with reason, we begin with feeling and insight. All of life is 99 percent nonrational. Reason is nothing compared to God's love. That's what makes us who we are. Reason is the first thing that should be dropped when you start exploring the spirit. You can bring reason to bear on what you find, but truth simply doesn't happen that way."

And the audience doesn't experience a play that way. They enter into the play by listening to the actors. "You can't dictate the outcome. You don't tell the audience what it should feel. You be it and let them react."

While actors learn the necessity of listening when they study their craft, others learn its importance when they study religion. Rabbi

Laurie Katz Braun has done both. As an actor and a playwright she had an understanding of the need for listening, and says that need also comes into play in Judaism where listening is so essential it is taught in the first prayer Jewish children learn, the *Shema*. "It's about 'Hear, O Israel. Listen up, Israel, God is your God.' " The command to listen, or giving ear, is repeated hundreds of times in the Torah, she says. "It's hard to have faith without listening. It allows you to get quiet, to listen to what's within and without. Building a relationship with God is about listening."

Braun studied English and theatre arts at the University of Pennsylvania, during which time she cofounded Stimulus Children's Theater, a traveling theatre that reaches out to children in the West Philadelphia community, and, with a grant from the B'nai B'rith Hillel Foundation, founded Teatron, the Jewish theatre company of the University of Pennsylvania. After graduating, instead of heading out on auditions, she chose a path that may seem far removed— studying at Hebrew Union College–Jewish Institute of Religion, where she earned a master's degree and rabbinic ordination. "As a young adult in college, I was devastated that I would have to choose between being an actor and a rabbi. I found out it was not possible to choose."

She didn't have to sacrifice one for the other because she found the perfect place to serve as a congregational rabbi, the Westchester Reform Temple in Scarsdale, New York, where most of the professional staff also had performing arts backgrounds and where she could work three-quarters time, using the other quarter to pursue her acting and theatrical writing careers. After three years of that arrangement she did make a choice, leaving the synagogue to pursue the theatre career, although she returned weekly for a year to teach. She says she could not function in either world without practicing the art of listening. "I define listening for myself as getting quiet. The other part of that is making space to get quiet, to build a space within where you are able to get quiet."

As a Jew, Braun says it's only natural to have a deep respect for listening. "In my religious tradition, listening is the first prayer. In the seventies we called the *Shema* the 'watchword for the faith.' It comes straight from Deuteronomy. It's the first prayer you teach a child because it's the prayer you say before sleep." The belief behind this, Braun says, is that one gives oneself up to God while sleeping, that one-sixtieth of the self dies and is with God. In the morning prayer, *modeh ani*, one expresses gratitude, "thanking God for returning your soul to you. I'm starting my day grounded and listening."

The *Shema* is also a prayer said twice in regular morning worship services, first as a blessing and then again, "like a proclamation," when the Torah is brought out. Braun sees this as embodying different ways of understanding listening. When the *Shema* is said the first time, worshipers cover their eyes, which "has a lot to do with listening and going inside." When the Torah is brought out, the prayer is said loudly. "Different ways of listening, same prayer," Braun says. A similar call to listen is behind the lighting of Shabbat candles on Friday night. "We thank God for a day of rest. We're listening and taking time out. These rituals are central to listening. They create moments of space and time when we have to listen."

Jewish commentary offers many different words all having to do with listening and hearing. In seminary she heard over and over again from her professors *simu lev,* which means listen or pay attention. "Literally it means put your heart into it," she says.

Another example of the relevance of listening to Jewish experience that Braun sees can be found in the Israeli national anthem, *HaTikvah*, which means "The Hope." "Hope requires listening; something beautiful is coming up. It reminds us we're connected to God. That's a key for actors, too. You can't face all that rejection without the hope this is sacred, meaningful work I'm doing."

While serving at the Westchester Reform Temple, Braun built a comprehensive youth program, including a teen theatre company, conducted teen healing services, and led teen dialogue groups.

Whenever they came to her with problems, she always encouraged them to be still and listen to their inner voices. This is just what her mentor does when she is stressed about something. Her mentor asks her: "Have you gotten quiet? Have you asked God? Have you listened?"

Braun tried to instill this practice in all her congregants. "As a rabbi, I care about what these people do when they leave. I know what they do when they're here." She tells them to listen to the divine. "This connects us with a sense of awe in the world. This is separate from organized religious life. To have an active spiritual, religious life is all about listening. This is so different from the lives we lead, with so much running around. If we didn't make time for listening, our spiritual lives would be really depleted. We're so caught up with technology and everything humanly made, the only way to connect with the divine is to separate and get quiet."

She says the best ways to learn to listen are to speak to God and then listen intuitively and to concentrate on one's breathing. "It's not as hard as it seems, but it requires a decision to be more conscious and to make time for it. It has to be a decision that you want a haven, a sacred space. I think it's that simple."

Listening in that sacred space led Braun to decide in 2001 to pursue acting and playwriting full-time. When she told her congregation she was leaving, she told them the *Shema* had been her guide. "I said, 'This is what I've been teaching your children for three years. What I need to do is take the next step on my journey, to be able to hear that.'"

Interestingly enough that next step landed her right back in a synagogue, only this time instead of as rabbi it was as playwright. As luck or divine intervention would have it, Braun met Rabbi Josh Simon at the 2002 Broadway Blessing, an interfaith service of song and scripture reading that brings the theatre community together every September to ask God's blessing on the new season. Simon was a participant representing Congregation Ezrath Israel/The Actors' Temple and Braun was in the audience. He was a newly appointed rabbi looking to reconnect his synagogue to its showbiz past; she was a newly unattached rabbi with a company, Theater 8, looking for a space.

"It was a *basherte* moment," Braun says. "It was meant to be. We were both at moments of time of new beginning. He was looking for a way to open the doors and revitalize the arts component of his synagogue, and we were looking for a home. This is bringing together the energy of Judaism and the creative arts."

The first work presented was Braun's play *Eighty-three Years*, a contemporary Jewish family drama about an expectant mother's decision over whether to name her child after her grandmother, as her grandmother ordered her to do before dying, or to give the child an identity of her own. Braun says the story is rooted in a conversation with her own grandmother. "The young woman's struggle is over how we form identities at every stage of our lives. What my grandmother said, 'I want my name to live on through you,' is a pretty powerful thing, but how much responsibility do we have to the next generation to find its own voice?"

For Braun, being an actor and being a rabbi have much in common. "They're both about telling the truth, tearing down and getting to what's most central. Listening is the key to success on both paths."

Both paths collided for her in 1993 in a significant way when she was a rabbinical student and was questioning whether she should continue. For the High Holy Days that year, she conducted a service for abused children, their families, and benefactors at a facility in California. One of those benefactors was a singer and former television host who had been immensely popular in the forties, fifties, and sixties, but with whom Braun, who was only twenty-two, was just vaguely familiar.

The way Braun included the children in the service and showed compassion for them impressed the singer, who told her own children about the young rabbinical student. When she died a short time later, her children asked Braun to conduct her funeral, saying they knew that's what their mother would have wanted.

Braun didn't even know how to conduct a Jewish funeral, but she met with the singer's children and listened as they shared stories about their mother, her generosity in charitable causes, and her love for her grandchildren, for whom she wrote and illustrated story-books. "I carry her with me every single day," Braun says. "She was a centered, light-filled person. I feel she transformed my life. It was as if she said, 'You're supposed to be a rabbi.' It was a profound moment of listening for me. You never know where it's going to come from."

Peter W. Culman, like Braun, also knows the necessity of listening in scripture and in theatre. As a homiletics professor at St. Mary's Seminary and University in Baltimore and for more than three decades managing director of Center Stage, the city's nationally esteemed regional theatre, he's had plenty of opportunity to reflect. "The Psalms continually advise us to look and listen. The reason why is because scripture came out of an oral tradition. Theatre histori-cally, as did religion, came out of that same insistence on learning to listen well."

Much of this has been lost in our culture, he says, because we can often just hit the rewind button to catch what we miss if our mind wanders. "There's no instant replay in theatre, thank God." There also are no two performances alike. "There can be rather considerable swings, and that can be as much because of the audience as because of the actors. If the audience is really attentive, that attention can pull the actors up, and the reverse also is true. That's no less true in church or a place of worship."

When asked for a definition of listening, Culman pauses awhile before coming up with one that captures the experience and not just the result of listening. "It's paying close attention to the spoken words and concurrently making certain I have nothing going on inside my brain that distracts this attention. There's an erased blackboard in my brain not allowing other information to appear. The words I'm hearing are the only words allowed to get on that blackboard."

It was Culman's mother who taught him the power of listening. After his father died of leukemia, Culman, his mother, and his brother moved into his aunt's house on the Upper East Side of Manhattan. She held formal dinner parties several times a week for guests who were expert conversationalists, listeners, and readers. His mother told him that in a good conversation handles are extended for the listener to grab. "You don't throw the ball back in conversation," she told him. Only ten, he didn't understand. She told him to listen very hard and he would begin to hear the handles.

He suggests four ways people can improve their listening skills. First, use "acknowledging grunts" or a single word spoken as a question, like *really?* or *oh?* to indicate you're hearing what the person is saying. Second, paraphrase what the person has just said and repeat it back. Third, ask a simple question that shows you are listening and want to hear more. Finally, if the speaker says something that dislodges a free association in your mind, honor that digression. "An opportunity for mutual energy of imagination occurs. It can lead to revelation in all kinds of ways."

This assumes one wants to listen to the other person. What about the people who are complainers, dull, or self-involved? Culman says to employ "the crap shoot of excellent will." By listening attentively, we can "up the ante" and get beyond the complaints and clichés. "There's a geyser in everyone that with the right circumstance will go off. We have the peculiar power to initiate that."

He offers two quotes to back this up. The first is from Quaker mystic Douglas Steere: "To listen another soul into a condition of disclosure and discovery may be almost the greatest service that any human being can perform for another." The second is from *Nonviolent Communication: A Language of Compassion* by Marshall B. Rosenberg: "Empathy is a respectful understanding of what others are experiencing. The Chinese philosopher Chuang-Tzu stated that true empathy requires listening with the whole being: 'The hearing that is only in the ears is one thing. The hearing of the understanding is another. But the hearing of the spirit is not limited to any one faculty, to the ear, or the mind. Hence it demands the emptiness of all the faculties. And when the faculties are empty, then the whole being listens. There is then a direct grasp of what is right there before you that can never be heard with the ear or understood with the mind.'"

Culman helps others develop strong listening skills through a consulting business for theatre professionals that he began after retiring from Center Stage in 2000. He places heavy emphasis on object exercises, requiring people to bring in something that is important to them and explain why. Through the sharing of listening and revelation, people learn more about each other and they develop compassion. "Then trust makes an entrance, and with trust you can do anything; but you've got to reach that point. Theatre is premised on collaboration, on the collective smarts, but you've got to begin with listening."

This is a rather unconventional approach to helping theatre staffs deal with raising more money and developing larger audiences. But if the saying is true that you can't argue with success, then you can't argue with Culman, who is largely responsible for making Center Stage, Maryland's state theatre, the financially sound theatre that it is. When he took over the fledgling theatre in 1966, it had a budget of $250,000 and eventually, even though the budget grew, an even higher deficit. When he left thirty-three years later, after a reign longer than that of any other managing director in the country, the budget was more than $5 million and he had built an endowment of more than $7 million. And he had kept the theatre in the black for two decades.

Culman is proof that the collaboration that can grow through listening makes good fiscal sense, but listening is also crucial to him as a Catholic. "Intentional listening comes out of the belief that the person you are listening to is God-filled. This is a loaded reason to make an extra effort to hear the person carefully because you will concurrently hear God if you are listening in that way."

Silence

For God alone my soul waits in silence;
from him comes my salvation.
~Psalm 62:1

I need a place where I can hide;
where no one sees my life inside.
~Marsha Norman, *The Secret Garden*

W AITING FOR GOD in silence is necessary because as
powerful as God is and as much as we celebrate God's
glory in prayer, liturgy, and ceremony, it is often only
in silence that we find God. The prophet Elijah discovered this in
chapter 19 of the Book of 1 Kings. "Go out and stand on the mountain before the Lord, for the Lord is about to pass by," he was told by
God. A great wind arose, "so strong that it was splitting mountains
and breaking rocks in pieces before the Lord, but the Lord was not
in the wind." An earthquake followed, "but the Lord was not in the
earthquake." Next came fire, but once again God was not present.
And then "a sound of sheer silence." God, making a great dramatic
entrance, came to Elijah in the most unexpected way.

The prophet Isaiah also reminds us of the significance of silence. "For thus said the Lord God, the Holy One of Israel: In returning and rest you shall be saved; in quietness and in trust shall be your strength."

Playwright Heather McDonald wrote of the connection between God and silence in her one-man play *An Almost Holy Picture*, which Kevin Bacon performed on Broadway in 2002. In the play, Samuel Gentle is an Episcopal priest who asks to be sent to a desert parish. "I was drawn there by light, space, the deep pleasure of unexpected life, and stillness," he says. "The geography allows for God. . . . Moses, Jeremiah, Jesus all spent time in the desert listening to the silence. And they brought back visions."

The Rev. Robert E. Kennedy, S.J., in his book *Zen Spirit, Christian Spirit: The Place of Zen in Christian Life*, writes: "There is a certain type of temperament which not only naturally inclines itself toward silent and reverent attention, but also longs for it. Those who possess this temperament longingly seek the deepening silence and are drawn to the intuitive moment that shakes their universe."

Phylicia Rashad is one of these people. "Silence is critical," she says. "Silence is crucial. Silence is necessary. It's mandatory. You've got to have silence." But you've got to work for it because "it's the one thing we don't have. There's always something going on."

Rashad works on finding her silence whether she's appearing on TV—she's best known for her role as Clair Huxtable on *The Cosby Show*—or onstage—she has appeared on and off Broadway and at regional theatres around the country. "Artists need silence because inspiration arises from silence. I've been watching very carefully this principle of silence and what it means. I've not experienced it yet to the extent I'd like to experience it, but it seems to grow in you if you pay attention to it."

In paying attention, Rashad has learned much about what true silence really is. "Silence is more than not speaking. It's internal, a state of mind. You could keep your mouth silent, but your mind could be going 99,000 miles a minutes. That's a lot of racket."

Often that racket comes from other people. In the summer of 2002 Rashad was on tour with Broadway Inspirational Voices, a gospel choir of theatre singer/actors. As the bus traveled through Arizona, New Mexico, and Colorado, she had to fight for her inner silence. "Our tour bus guide was very enthusiastic about her work as a tour guide. She wanted to explain every rock, every blade of grass, and every cloud in the sky and to direct our attention to them all the time. I respected her enthusiasm, but I thought, 'How am I going to get through this?'"

What she did was look out the window and focus on the changes in the landscape as the plains gave way to the Rocky Mountains. "I realized how quiet it was out there. It was so quiet." The kind of quiet she continues to draw from. "I think about that and just thinking about it I get quiet inside."

She also practices siddha meditation for an hour every day, calling it "a path of grace," a path she has been following since 1980. "It stills the tendencies of the mind. You watch your breathing. By paying close attention, it begins to even out. When the breath evens out, the mind becomes still."

Keeping the mind still helps one weather the highs and lows of show business, and Rashad knows them as well as any performer. She got her first taste of the limelight when she was eleven and was chosen to narrate at a citywide music festival in her native Houston, Texas. From that experience she knew she wanted to be an actor. She appeared in school plays and went on to Howard University in Washington, D.C., where she majored in theatre arts, graduating magna cum laude.

After moving to New York, she got parts Off-Broadway with the Negro Ensemble Company and at the Henry Street Settlement and

Off, Off-Broadway, sometimes for no money. For two years she shared an apartment with her younger sister, the actor, director, and choreographer Debbie Allen.

In 1973 she landed on Broadway as one of twelve munchkins in *The Wiz*. In a Lifetime TV *Intimate Portrait* about Rashad, *Wiz* musical supervisor Harold Wheeler said she stood out. "She always had that star quality about her, even as a munchkin in the chorus." Unfortunately this wasn't enough to move her into a starring role. After three and a half years as first understudy to play Glinda, she was passed over in favor of the second understudy. She stayed on in the chorus, but when it happened again, this time after a year understudying a lead in *Dreamgirls*, she quit.

She became a regular in 1983 on *One Life to Live*, playing ambitious publicist Courtney Wright. And then luck and leading lady status came her way in the role of Clair Huxtable. Rashad's chemistry with Bill Cosby was seen as a contributing factor in the show's success—it ran on NBC for eight years, from 1984 to 1992, and was the number one show in the country for five of those years.

Meditation was an important part of her life during those heady days, but so was theatre. When the television writers' strike halted production for twenty-two weeks in 1988, she replaced Bernadette Peters as The Witch in the original Broadway production of *Into the Woods*. And after Cosby folded the TV show in 1992, she returned to Broadway as Sweet Anita in *Jelly's Last Jam* and has continued to work in theatre.

During one of these appearances, when she was starring as Peggy Clark, a former big-city model married to a small-town undertaker in the Off-Broadway production of *Blue*, she met Michael McElroy, founder and director of Broadway Inspirational Voices, who was playing a former lover. Through McElroy, she found a way to deepen her connection between theatre and spiritual centering—she joined his gospel choir. "I like gospel music and being with creative people and people who are good at what they do," she says. "The people in Broadway Inspirational Voices are the best."

Although the music is different from that in the Episcopal Church into which she was christened, she connected with gospel music the first time she heard it as a child. "I said, 'Oh my goodness.' The energy, the feeling, the devotion are so powerful in that sound."

Paradoxically, it helps her maintain her stillness. "The right kinds of sounds can lead you to silence. It takes you inside yourself."

She thinks everyone has a quiet place inside, but that actors are often better at finding it. "For performing artists, it's the nature of our work to 'tap in.' Artists' work is really internal. That creates an awareness." People in other professions think outside themselves, she says, adding that some artists do too, "but you can tell the difference."

Tapping in is a regular part of her acting preparation. "As a performer, I don't like to talk a lot before a performance. I like to be quiet and feel inside. I become available to the creative energy inside myself that's doing the work. I have to be available to myself, spontaneous. But that doesn't happen if I'm not quiet inside, if I'm distracted and my thoughts are all over the place."

And this inward dwelling continues onstage and after the curtain goes down. "The goal is to establish oneself in this state. It's not something you return to—it's something you never leave." But it's not an escape from reality, she emphasizes. "It's being in the world more fully present. You're not out of the world. You move to a source inside. We're in the world for a reason. Let's really be in it. Let's find out what it *really* means to be in it."

The idea that silence and daily activity can go hand in hand is not as contradictory as it sounds because, as Rashad points out, silence is more than not speaking. It can, in fact, be an essential part of language, often its climax. In the theatre, the "sound of sheer silence" can be used for dramatic effect as a way of suggesting mounting tension. Harold Pinter's much-commented-on use of pauses reflects his interest in silence. "Life is much more mysterious than plays make it out to be," he said. "And it is the mystery which fascinates me; what happens between the words, what happens when no words are spoken at all."

Time between words is not downtime for the actor, says Edward Herrmann, who has made use of that time onstage, film and television. "You don't die onstage while you're listening," he said in a 1983 interview in the *New York Times*. "You don't just wait until the others are finished speaking until you begin. You are going through a process of change in your silence. Actors move not from speech to speech but through a whole experience."

Herrmann compares his appreciation for the use of silence in acting to the unfolding of nature, which teaches him to slow down in his work. He lives on eight acres in Salisbury, Connecticut, where he restores himself from his busy work life, which includes frequent trips back and forth between Connecticut and California for his role in *Gilmore Girls* and other TV and film work. "It's as much nature as I have time to assimilate. I watch the birds at the feeder and watch the way the flowers bud. This irresistible power takes time. When it arrives, it's overwhelming."

When his schedule permits, he escapes to his summer home in Michigan where in the early 1990s he created a chapel, or "meditation cell," out of a sauna built on the property by the previous owner, a Quaker. In addition to being a prayer haven, it has served as a recording studio; when he was recording the Dodge account, he used the space for the microphone and sound cones.

Now, however, its chief purpose is sacred. Herrmann divided the building into two rooms, put in fir floors and lined the walls of the smaller room with cedar planks. In this room he hung an eighteenth-century French crucifix and dozens of icons—one Greek, a few Serbian, the rest Russian. "They number over twenty-five, I think, and when all the lampada are lighted it is a lovely spiritual blaze," he says. In addition, this room has at least four good-sized reliquaries (containers in which sacred relics are kept) holding "some fifty-odd saints." Other features of this sacred space include a wall dedicated to St. Thérèse, an icon devoted to the last czar and his family, and a photograph of Muktananda, an Indian mystic Herrmann met in India in 1965, who "enjoys the company of saints and angels." Two small windows, one on the north wall and one on the south, bracket the east wall where the majority of the icons and the crucifix hang. The larger room has a small fireplace; his desk and bookcase, filled mostly with religious and philosophy books; and an easy chair. Close to a dozen icons are hung here as well. This office has white walls and three large windows that allow him to take in the nature that surrounds him. "All in all, I'm a very lucky Christian to have such a place of retreat. Virtually no one comes here except me. It's a very private place."

Herrmann appreciates the time alone to pray, read, or observe nature. That kind of silence and reflection also are at work for an actor in developing a dramatic part, he says. "In rehearsal you wait and let things pop up before you jump on them. It's about waiting. You need to let the juice from the roots flow up and not force it. You let it happen."

That energy of silence is necessary for actors both onstage and off. "Silence onstage can be incredibly powerful," Liam Neeson says. And offstage, it is a force to be reckoned with. "You have to be very still and listen to accept silence, to be content with it. Some people it freaks. They have to go into themselves and they're afraid of what they may confront."

Growing up in a small house in a government-run project in Northern Ireland with his parents and three sisters, Neeson cultivated a sense of privacy. He jokes now that he could be content sitting and watching paint dry. Seriously, he would like to go on a silent retreat. He was supposed to make one in Wales years ago, but a scheduling change interfered. "We're all always acting. You need to be able to sit in silence and not beat up on yourself. It's hard to say to yourself, 'You are human. Welcome to the human race.'"

That sitting in silence also has its place in the theatre because of the sense of the unexpected in silence that makes it an effective device in drama. Although it seems more fitting for contemplation than theatre, silence "is really the key in some respects" to the work of Matt Mitler's experimental theatre ensemble, DZIECI, which he founded in 1997. (The name means "children" in Polish.) Members of the company, which describes itself as "dedicated to a search for the 'sacred' through the medium of theatre," come together in silence before and after performances. They also rely on their practice of inner silence to see them through visits to the elderly, children with psychiatric problems, and others in hospital settings. These visit/performances are required for DZIECI members, but they could be draining without the spiritual practice of silence, Mitler says. This practice includes each person stepping back from time to time throughout the visits, which can be day-long, to evaluate herself or himself, what Mitler calls taking a picture of himself. "I turn my attention inward to observe what is actually happening inside this vessel that is my body. It's like balancing a bowl of water on my head and that bowl of water is energy."

The goal is not only not to spill all the energy at the hospital, but to possibly have even more energy as a result of such attention. "That part of the work is a sacred process," Mitler says. "Being quiet is being more balanced." Drawing on inner silence helps him deal with any patient, even those who may appear unpleasant. "If I approach them intellectually, it distances me. If it is with my whole person, I find immense compassion and I'm able to do something, but it doesn't come from me. I'm as touched as they are."

Mitler's personal practice of silence includes meditating each morning and returning to that quiet throughout the day, using often irritating experiences like riding the subway or standing in a bank line to practice centering.

Silence as a centering technique is not unusual, but hours of silence as theatre is. So when members of DZIECI invited the public to "Vow of Silence," a four-hour workshop during which no talking would be allowed, they had no idea what to expect. Their goal was to explore inner and outer silence, and, like all DZIECI workshops, they started with the theme and then followed the nature of the group participating, assisting them to "moments of transformation."

The setting for "Vow of Silence" was a sixteenth-floor rehearsal studio on Eighth Avenue in Manhattan. DZIECI members met their guests outside the room to inform them that the silence could not be broken. If they needed to talk to a member of the company, they should motion for the person to come outside. Mitler, who initially trained in humanistic and existential psychology and group process, was the director, moving the afternoon from one experience to another with subtle gestures.

"One thing I like to have is a lot of waiting, but not in an anxious way like for a bus," Mitler told the ensemble before guests arrived. Luckily the workshop participants seemed at ease with both the silence and the waiting, gathering in a circle at first to just stand still, with the only sound that of the whirring of the heating system. After several minutes, Mitler took a few steps to the side; others did the same. This was followed by head rolling, then winging of arms until the movements began to flow in a circle. The silence was broken only by the sounds of knees cracking and heavy breathing as the pace quickened. The movements began to resemble a choreographed dance.

With the group thus unified, Mitler knelt on the floor, signaling the start of the trust exercises in which ensemble members and eventually guests climbed on one another's shoulders and were lifted to touch the ceiling, before falling backwards into the arms of the waiting group. One guest broke the silence at this point with a sigh of ecstasy when she landed safely. The session ended in a circle with a ritualized meal, with a DZIECI member washing the guests' hands and another drying. Mitler motioned for people to begin feeding each other, which they did before leaving in silence.

Outside the room, guests were eager to talk about their experiences, but DZIECI members tried to help them control their energy. "It's our responsibility to assist the people we work with in maintaining their connection to this energy as long as possible," Mitler says. "We're not just there for a high experience. We assist a change of being so something can linger."

The fact that silence has the power to lead to such a change of being is no surprise to people in religious life. Rabbi James L. Mirel says silence is "a center of Jewish tradition," rooted in the scriptures. "Silence is the beginning of wisdom, according to the Book of Proverbs. One is enjoined to have a silent response to the universe." Ecclesiastes makes it clear there is a time to speak, but also a time to keep silent. "Be silent before God, silent before those who are more wise and silent before the elders."

And be silent in the face of pain and suffering inflicted upon you. In the Book of Job, after Job has challenged God about the great misfortunes that have come his way, he says he will put his finger to my lips and remain silent. "Don't speak in front of that which is greater than you," says Mirel, who serves Temple B'nai Torah in Bellevue, Washington, a suburb of Seattle, and is a co-author of *Stepping Stones to Jewish Spiritual Living.*

Silent prayer and meditation are the best ways to listen to God, which all Jews are commanded to do in the *Shema*, the primary prayer of Judaism, which states, "Listen, O Israel: Adonai is our God, Adonai alone." Mirel says silence is needed to follow this order. "It says listen Israel, not speak, but listen."

Silence helps one develop a sense of wonder and awe at the vastness and complexity of the world and all the gifts we've been given, Mirel says. "Judaism has a reverence for the universe and God. Words are central to the ritual life of Judaism, but silence can be a stronger place to be. It's more a state of being." The state of being in silence can bring peace not only to one's self, but to others "by not imposing one's sounds on the universe," Mirel says. "We have wonderful ways of speaking words, making music and poetry, but they are enhanced when they are interspersed with silence."

Mirel is a music-maker himself, playing bass in a klezmer band. (Klezmer is dance music that originated in Eastern Europe and is a joyful sound associated with weddings and celebrations.) He plays at area nursing homes, in Christian churches in the Seattle area as a way of introducing non-Jews to this music, at Jewish weddings and occasionally at services in his synagogue. "Music is a balance between sound and silence," he says.

Silence also can be effective in relationships and is often best when one doesn't know what to say. "Words have the chance of being misused. When in doubt, remain silent." Silence also can be "the ultimate expression of romantic love." And while it can enhance human relationships in this way, it is a powerful tool in our ultimate relationship. "We don't have the privilege of hearing God's voice the way people in ancient times did. Silence is the best way to be in relationship with God. God is silent, so we need to be silent."

Mirel says one of the greatest gifts we can give ourselves is to recognize we are not essential for the universe to continue. We can turn off cell phones for an hour or go away on a silent retreat for several days. "There's a humility that comes from knowing that if you are not in communication for an hour, the world will go on. If we remove ourselves for an hour or a few days, life will go on."

People need to make a conscious decision to set aside thirty minutes or an hour each day. Silent retreats are also possible for Jews, even though Judaism calls for saying prayers communally at set times each day. "Prayers can be gentle or quiet. Praying is not considered an interruption of silence." And although "Judaism believes God doesn't need too much praise," putting more emphasis as it does on doing good deeds, silence can help people in determining the focus of their actions. "Silence is a good way to use your time. It enhances your future in terms of giving you direction for what you should be doing."

Mirel cites the Jewish mystical tradition of "clinging to God," or *devekut*. "We want to approach as close as we can. In life we have limited access to God, so we try ways of clinging, of being in contact with God. Meditation and silence are primary ways of going above and beyond everyday existence to the spiritual world. We want to peek through the curtain that separates the material world and the spiritual world to be in touch with God."

Sr. Mary Elizabeth Earley, a member of the Sisters of Charity of New York, had similar feelings about the power of and need for silence. "I don't think you can have a spiritual life if you don't have a good bit of silence in your life. It leads to reflection, to self-knowledge, to prayer. It can be a very powerful shaping experience in your life."

Earley learned this as a young woman. Although her religious order is an active rather than contemplative one, it still gave a great deal of attention to silence. "When I entered almost sixty years ago, we were still in our old-fashion mode. There were many places in the house where we never spoke and many times of the day. There was silence at meals and in the morning until after breakfast. It was something built into our lives, more than you would think in an order with a great deal of activity. It makes a difference."

Earley led quite an active life with her order. Among her endeavors, she taught English for many years at Cathedral High School in Manhattan; the College of Mount Saint Vincent in Riverdale, New

York; and the University of Bethlehem—the only Catholic university in the West Bank—and served as academic dean at the former Seton College in South Yonkers, New York. She also wrote two volumes of her community's history, covering the years from 1960 to 1996.

But she never lost her appreciation for silence. Trusting in its great power, she gave herself over to it for an entire year following eight years on the governing board at the College of Mount Saint Vincent. "It was one of the best years of my life. After eight years of meetings and constant phone calls, all I wanted to do was escape." She chose a hermitage in Kentucky owned by the Sisters of Loretto. Surrounded by seven hundred acres of farmland, she had a little house in the woods where she lived for a year, attending daily liturgy at the main house but never talking to anyone. Descriptions of that sacred time eluded her.

"It's hard to translate in so many words. What I learned is that silence leads into a great sense of peace. God does dwell within each one of us, but he's not intrusive, or she's not. You're not in touch with that reality unless you bring yourself to quiet within yourself. You become aware that you are spirit and you come in touch with God."

She also lived for three years in a House of Prayer, part of a movement within the Catholic Church in which members of a religious community establish a contemplative dimension in their home by opening it for retreats and spiritual direction. At Earley's House of Prayer they also practiced yoga and studied Eastern spirituality.

After retirement, Earley lived in the convent on the grounds of the College of Mount Saint Vincent, grounds which the college acquired in the 1860s from Edwin Forrest, a renowned Shakespearean actor of the day. Her building overlooked the Hudson River, somewhat apart from the main campus, so Earley was still able to enjoy silence. But when she walked around the campus, she realized even more what a gift her early experience had been. "I almost never pass a student who's not on the phone. That would be like an enslavement to me. I see it on buses, trains, everywhere I go. It says something about a lack of inner resources.

"They've never had a taste of silence. It's an acquired taste. You let quiet seep into you. You become acclimated to silence." She lived with nearly fifty sisters and never even heard a radio or TV. "That's the kind of life sisters have led. You have to learn how to be silent, I've discovered. It's something of an art. You learn by opportunity."

She never forgot a fellow novice's reaction to the nighttime silence when they were both new to religious life. "She said silence brought closure to that day and whatever went on. It was starting a whole new page the next day. It was a buffer, so the day was fresh when you started it."

Being comfortable with silence is harder for some people, but it can be acquired, she said. "In our life it was a rule. There has to be some kind of attraction in it for you, but people can be taught the meaning of silence and how to use it. You learn by practice. That's what we did. When you come to the convent as a young woman, you're not used to having silence. You come to treasure it, but it's hard at first. It's a discipline." She suggested people set aside time each day in which they create quiet. "See what it can do for you. It can grow and bring inner peace."

Spending time with nature also helps. "The natural world, for the most part, is silent. There's a difference between sound and noise. The sound of trees, water, and wind can all be a part of silence. It's deeply embedded in the natural world, a world we are a part of, and it's deeply embedded in us. Everything grows in silence."

Christians can understand the importance of silence by reading in the gospels how often Jesus went off alone to pray. In the first chapter of St. Mark's gospel, Jesus drove an unclean spirit from a man in the synagogue, after which he entered the house of his apostle Simon and cured his mother-in-law of a fever. That evening "the whole city was gathered around the door" and he cured many people. "In the morning, while it was still very dark, he got up and went out to a deserted place, and there he prayed." Time and again this is how the gospels say he renewed himself, most dramatically in his forty days and forty nights in the desert.

Earley said she had a new appreciation of these experiences in Jesus' life when she lived in the Holy Land from 1982 through 1987 while teaching at the University of Bethlehem. "Living there was a truly wonderful experience. You do have the sense of what it means to live in the desert." She felt a sense of inner quiet looking at the stars and the sun, knowing they were in the same trajectory Jesus saw and walking on the roads built over the old walking trails he traveled. "To live in these places over time is quite different. It's a great privilege."

She also understood the Desert Fathers who, in the fourth through sixth centuries, fled the corrupt world of the Roman Empire, which was Christian in name but more pagan in practice, to imitate Jesus' experience in the desert. This appreciation of silence is at the core of the great religious communities like the Benedictines and Trappists, at the core of Catholicism itself, she said. "All the great religious orders are founded on silence. They are the ones who gave birth to that tremendous heritage. It's an absolutely fundamental tradition in the Church. Knowledge of God is deeply related to silence. Silence is deeply, deeply at the heart of Catholicism."

She couldn't imagine it any other way. "When you want to learn something, what do you do? You usually have a silent time when you study or examine something. You do your best when you're quiet."

And you become your best.

"Silence is alive. It's a living reality, pregnant with all kinds of possibilities of coming in touch with what up until now is beyond you. It's moving into depth."

Author's note: Sr. Mary Elizabeth entered eternal life five months after this interview. At her funeral Mass, Msgr. John Farley read an account of one of her experiences in the Holy Land, which she had written about in a volume of her congregation's history. When she broke her ankle one day while walking in the desert, a young Israeli guide with a group of German tourists ran to a Bedouin camp and persuaded them to lend a donkey. The ancient Bedouin woman who returned with him snapped Sister's dislocated ankle back into place, then took off her veil, tore it into strips, dipped them into the icy water of an aqueduct and wrapped the swelling ankle. Two Israeli soldiers on holiday with their girl-friends had stopped to help. "The soldier lifted me onto the donkey, but I was not able to keep my seat, not being accustomed to bareback rides. The old woman held me on one side and the soldier on the other, as we covered the treacherous miles to the monastery. Although this was not a moment for theo-logical speculation, I could not help but be aware that we were traveling on the road from Jerusalem to Jericho, a most unlikely trio: an American nun, a Bedouin Arab and an Israeli soldier. It was a situation somewhat reminiscent of the one described 2,000 years ago. It gave me hope for the land in which blind hate seemed to dominate most of the time."

I believe Sr. Mary Elizabeth is praying for peace, and praying for us. I am reminded of the words of Albert Schweitzer: "No ray of sunshine is ever lost, but the green which it awakes into existence needs time to sprout, and it is not always granted for the sower to see the harvest. All work that is worth anything is done in faith."

Prayer

Therefore let all who are faithful offer prayer to you;
at a time of distress, the rush of mighty waters
shall not reach them.
~PSALM 32:6

God on high, hear my prayer.
In my need, you have always been there.
~HERBERT KRETZMER, *Les Misérables*

PRAYER IS a spiritual practice well suited to actors, and everyone else for that matter, because of its versatility. It can be active, as in letting your life be prayer, or it can be contemplative, as in meditation or scripture reflection. It can be done with standard prayers like the *Shema* or the Lord's Prayer, or it can be made up. Prayers can be said throughout the day, like the *berakah*, expressions of thanks that Jews ideally say at least one hundred times a day, or they can be practiced at set times, as in the Jewish custom of *keva*, routine prayers said morning, afternoon, and evening, or the Liturgy of the Hours (also known as the Divine Office), the Christian monastic tradition of praying at specific hours from sunrise to sunset. For many, reading or reciting Psalms is a calming form of prayer, as is walking a labyrinth, a spiritual practice that is enjoying a new round of popularity. The labyrinth, a sacred circle with a single path leading to its center, dates at least to the Middle Ages, when designs were fashioned into the floors of cathedrals. It was a way for the faithful to make a prayerful pilgrimage at a time when it was too dangerous and costly for them to travel to the Holy Land. Walking the path can bring tranquillity to the soul, opening it up to prayer and meditation.

To St. Augustine, singing was a door to prayer. He believed to sing was to pray twice. St. Elizabeth Ann Seton, the first American-born saint, said: "Without prayer I should be of little service to others." She described prayer as "a habit of lifting up the heart to God, as in a constant communication with Him."

In the twentieth century, Evelyn Underhill, an Anglican mystic, wrote: "We must accustom our attention, that wanders over all other interests, to fix itself on Him. Such deliberate attention to God is the beginning of real prayer. Prayer is never to be judged by feeling that goes with it; it is the willed intercourse of our tiny spirits with the Infinite Spirit of Love." Like many others, she believed in the merging of action and contemplation, that "every bit of work done toward God is a prayer."

Learning to look at work as prayer is something Liam Neeson discovered in the jungles of Colombia, South America, while filming *The Mission*, a 1986 movie about eighteenth-century Jesuits. "I was at a crossroads in my life," he says. "I was reasonably successful as an actor. I was thirty-two or thirty-three with a potential career ahead of me. I had done some flimflam movies, but I didn't understand what being an actor meant anymore."

He liked the downtime, "getting drunk at night and getting laid as much as I could," to which he adds, "I was single at the time." But for the classically trained stage actor, something was missing. "The work side was easy. It was no big stretch."

He had let slip the Roman Catholic faith he had been raised in in Ballymena, a predominantly Protestant town in Northern Ireland near Belfast, which contributed to his feelings of being at a crossroads. As research for *The Mission*, he read *The Jesuits* by J. C. Aveling and *Theology of Liberation* by Gustavo Gutierrez. He also became friends with the Rev. Daniel Berrigan, S.J., a technical advisor for the film who "told me extraordinary stories of his life and the life of a Jesuit."

Through his Jesuit research Neeson made a discovery that deeply affected his outlook. He learned about the Spiritual Exercises of Jesuit founder St. Ignatius Loyola who encouraged his students to study scripture by taking the part of a character in a Bible story, such as a shepherd in the stable at Bethlehem, and employing all the senses to imaginatively enter into the scene. Neeson recognized the connection between the Spiritual Exercises and Konstantin Stanislavsky's *An Actor Prepares*, which deals with the profound process an actor should go through to present a part onstage.

"I found out in the jungles of South America that Stanislavsky had based his technique on the Spiritual Exercises. It was a real revelation to me, and it brought two big parts of my life together. The Irish Catholic side was married to the life of an actor and I found out acting could be a form of prayer. It helped me knowing that. It was like a little godsend message." Now he uses that form of prayer for others. "I offer my performance as prayer for someone I've worked with as an actor or someone who has died. The image that comes into my head as I walk to the stage, I offer that performance up for that person."

Acting as prayer is enhanced by the fact that theatre actors must perform their parts over and over, he says. "It becomes like a mantra. The more you repeat it, the more it reveals its secrets. You really enter into that world. When you're doing it eight times a week, twice on Wednesdays and Saturdays, you can get in touch with something quite extraordinary."

What seemed like a revelation when he was in the jungle actually had its roots in that Irish Catholicism of his childhood. Christened William John Neeson, his family called him Liam in honor of a local priest. For six years he was an altar boy, "getting up at all hours for Mass with only the priest and two old ladies in the church." Even though it was hard rising early and heading out into a cold morning in northeastern Ireland, the experience affected him deeply. "There was always something really powerful, which I've never forgotten. The putting on of vestments and lighting candles, it's a wonderful ritual that never changes from one Mass to another. It helped fashion me to want to be an actor."

He appeared in school plays and at festivals around Ireland, while still pursuing another interest—boxing, for which he achieved the status of Ulster youth heavyweight champion. A broken nose when he was fifteen didn't stop him from continuing, but blackouts and memory loss did. He attended Queen's University in Belfast for a year before transferring to a teaching college in Newcastle, which he left after two years. Stints as an architect's clerk and forklift operator followed while he was in his early twenties. In 1976, on a dare from a coworker, he called the Lyric Players Theatre in Belfast. The owner just happened to be looking for an actor his age and height—six feet, four inches—so he auditioned and got the part.

After two years he joined the Abbey Theatre in Dublin. It was during that time he landed his first movie role, as Sir Gawain in *Excalibur* in 1980. He went on to work in London and Hollywood before making his Broadway debut in *Anna Christie* in 1993 opposite Natasha Richardson, whom he married in July 1994. That role, as seaman Mat Burke, earned him a Tony Award nomination. It also landed him the role that made him a star, that of Oskar Schindler in Steven Spielberg's *Schindler's List*, for which he was nominated for an Academy Award. He was nominated for another Tony in 2002 for his performance as John Proctor in a revival of *The Crucible*.

Living now in New York and continuing to act in movies and onstage, he attends Mass occasionally and says his faith is different from that of his altar boy years. "I question more now. I don't mean that it's all hokum, but I've lost a simple faith. I do still believe, but I like to encompass all religions now. I believe we're all paying homage to God."

But churchgoing is still a part of his life. "I always drop in a church when passing to say my Catholic prayers, and I make sure my children say them." He is raising his two sons Catholic because "they should learn some roots in a certain dogma. Not The One True Church, but I tell them there was a man called Jesus Christ who was the Son of God, simple stories, that he was a man the world is still figuring who he is." Churches are "comforting places," he says. "Generally I just give thanks for how lucky I am. I'm healthy, I have some money in the bank, I have healthy children and a wonderful wife."

Vanessa Williams also thanks God for her blessings. "When I'm alone I pray before sleep. It's a prayer of thanks that gives me clarity and makes me feel a sense of calm. I'm thankful for all my blessings. I have four healthy children, the career I've always wanted, a husband who adores me, my parents are living. I ask God to protect my family and friends and ask for good health. I never pray 'I want this part'; I pray to be guided and then it gets done."

Like Neeson, she is raising her children Catholic, at St. John and St. Mary Church in Chappaqua, New York, the Westchester County town where they live. "People my age who might have had problems with the church are coming back as parents. I feel there's a need to have faith in life. It's nice to see people reappear and now feel accepted in a way they might not have twenty or thirty years ago."

She says St. John and St. Mary is a great parish, and she likes the touches like a glassed-in crying room where parents can go with their babies and still see and hear the Mass. "The Church has changed tremendously. The Mass used to be in Latin and kids were not allowed to be vocal. The Mass was not tailored to kids. It's more accommodating now, more friendly, with a lot more humor. It's less intimidating." Like Neeson, she loves praying in the tradition and ritual of the Catholic Mass. "What I love is that even in different parishes you can still feel connected."

When she is in Los Angeles where her husband, Rick Fox, is a forward on the Lakers basketball team, she worships at Our Lady of Malibu. For her it's a relaxing change from East Coast liturgies; with its acoustic guitar and flute it's "like progressive jazz." For her children the holding of hands for the Lord's Prayer and raising them overhead is awkward, but she helps them find meaning in the worship. "I love being able to take the kids and have discussions after about what they noticed and what they missed."

As a child, Williams had a different experience of going to Mass. Her mother was the organist at St. Theresa's, their parish in Briarcliff Manor, New York. "I have many memories up there in the balcony turning pages for my mother or watching weddings; I loved to look at what the bride was wearing. It was very rarely we all worshiped as a family; on holidays we did. Most of the time I was next to my mom at the organ."

For most of her acting career Williams has been a cast member, so when she took her first stab at being an executive producer—for the Lifetime film *The Courage to Love*—she felt free to bring her prayer life to the set. The movie is about the life of Henriette Delille who, in antebellum New Orleans, founded the Sisters of the Holy Family to serve the poor and elderly. For Williams, telling Delille's story was a way to draw attention not only to the work of Catholic religious women but also to the lives of black Catholics. "I'm a black Catholic and I don't see a lot of black Catholics in the media. There's a tendency to think all blacks are Southern Baptists." With Delille's life, Williams found a story about a woman of color who was Catholic and had a calling. "I felt compelled to do it."

She had originally planned to play the older sister, afraid that because of her glamorous image she would not be taken seriously as a nun. But Lifetime wanted her in the lead, so she trusted Delille's spirit to guide her. "I have never been more involved in a story. I got the chance to take the idea on paper and work on it with the screenwriter and to choose the director."

Because she didn't want Delille's religious story to get watered down by the commercial demands of television, she took time on the set before the cameras rolled on the first day to hold a moment of silence and then offer a prayer asking Delille to bring everyone together. She prayed they would do justice to her story and that Delille would continue watching over them. "I knew she would because she had brought us so far. I felt blessed."

The project did seem to be blessed—from the time of original discussion of the idea to getting it on paper, casting, acquiring funding, lining up commitment from Lifetime, and getting the cameras rolling, it took only about a year, a remarkably short time. Williams said her brain had told her it would be hard to sell a story about a nun, but Lifetime "jumped aboard and it was eerily easy."

Her portrayal of Delille and her efforts at getting the movie made earned her a 2002 MIRA Award. MIRA (both an acronym for Media Images & Religious Awareness and the Spanish word for "look") was started in the early 1990s by sisters from communities in New York and New Jersey to counter shallow images of nuns in films and on television. Her commitment to her parish helped in the moviemaking; she received support from her pastor at St. John and St. Mary, Msgr. Timothy McDonnell, who has since become an auxiliary bishop of the New York archdiocese. McDonnell helped her with content and answered questions.

Williams says she has not met the sisters of Delille's community, who still minister in New Orleans. She would like to visit with her daughters Jillian and Melanie, who appeared in the movie as children Delille was teaching in opposition to the laws of the day. She also hopes Delille will be honored one day as a saint for her courage. "She had to fight against racism, the hierarchy of the Catholic Church, and what society said she was supposed to do as a Quadroon (mixed race) woman. She used her courage. That's what I have to do as a woman of color."

That may include doing more work with religious themes. "I have no problem incorporating religion into a story because it affects almost everything, either positively or negatively."

Michael McElroy is another singer/actor who has no trouble incorpo-rating religion—and prayer—into his professional life. "Let's have our prayer and get to work," he tells members of Broadway Inspirational Voices, the gospel choir of theatre performers he founded in 1993. They were gathered at the Shetler Studios on Eighth Avenue for a four-hour rehearsal for *Grace*, the choir's first full-length CD. "Stand, please," said McElroy, who waited at the front of the room before an upright piano.

With that, the nearly three dozen singers became silent. In the bare-bones studio rented for their rehearsal, they paused to turn their atten-tion to God. "Join hands with the person next to you," McElroy said, and soon all were united, their heads bowed. "Thank you for the opportunity to gather once more and praise you with this incredible music. Clear our minds and hearts to approach this music in the purest way. Help us to focus the way you want us to go and not the way we want to go." He told God the music touches them and thanked God for letting them offer praise in that way. "I just thank you for the joy to do this." At times choir members responded with a quiet but enthusiastic "Amen" or "Yes!" "We give you the honor and praise and glory," McElroy said in conclusion.

Prayer ended, he became all business. "We have lots to do so I don't want to compete with talking," he said as he handed out music to the first song, "He Always Answers Prayer for Me." He directed the sopranos, then the altos, tenors and basses, having them go over it and over it until he was pleased: "I can't tell you how to pray. I don't know the words to say, but I know my Savior cares, and his spirit always meets me there," they sang.

McElroy wanted the prayer of this song to be perfect. "I'm not con-vinced," he told them repeatedly. This was the first of several rehearsals for the group's CD, and McElroy didn't want to waste a minute. As pres-sured as he may have felt, though, nothing could interfere with that time at the beginning. He and the choir pray together before every rehearsal and each concert, thanking God for the opportunity to come together and for the talents given them. "We ask that God sustain us and allow the music to glorify him and to work healing in our lives," McElroy says.

They also pray during concerts. During the fall 2002 fundraiser at the Church of St. Mary the Virgin in Times Square, McElroy told people in the packed pews that no matter whether they had come with heavy or joyful hearts, "there's a blessing here for you." And throughout the evening audience members seemed to feel it, rising to their feet, applauding, stomping, and shouting out thanks to God, McElroy, and the choir.

A blessing is also exactly what Bertilla Baker found in the music when she joined the choir in the late 1990s. "I was at a low point in my life that had really brought me to my knees in prayer. I begged God to help me make it through and give me faith."

God answered that prayer by connecting her with McElroy. Her father had died and her marriage had ended. Leaving her husband after five years was hard, but he had relapsed into addictions and she needed to leave. She had left her showbiz career to work in the antique business with him in Canada, but she could no longer stay. "I just left everything in Canada. I had to start all over again. I had no money and no job."

Then God entered in. She had made a demo tape of Keith Thompson's song "I Will Walk with Jesus," which found its way to McElroy, who called her and asked her to join his choir. "As divine order would have it, I didn't actively pursue it, but I was meant to be in the choir. When Michael called I jumped at the chance. He came into my life when I was at a huge crossroads. I was extremely grateful. I knew it was going to be wonderful."

And it has been. Singing in the choir has been healing, and Baker has turned it into a form of prayer. She also discovered another form of prayer to help her through. "I decided in this spiritual recovery from all these traumas to practice gratitude."

She remembers sitting in her living room one day feeling "so sad and depressed." She focused on the coffee table, observing the grain, and was filled with reverence for God for creating the beautiful wood. She then studied her hands, the "ten fingers that move and do something for me," the lines in her skin, and rejoiced in "the miracle of that creation." Guiding her thoughts toward thankfulness changed her mood entirely, so much so that she began writing her thoughts in a "book of gratitude." "I keep it by my bedside," she says. "I try to focus my life on all the blessings I have instead of the things I want and think I need. I focus on the abundance and try to live according to God's plan. This brings more abundance into your life."

A third factor helping her through that time was watching Charles Stanley's *In Touch Ministries* on television. But most crucial of all was that she trusted God. "I just prayed for faith. To this day that has been my chief prayer." That prayer keeps her going through all the rejections and spells without work. "Actors are so in touch with that because we have so much uncertainty in our careers. To be a performing artist is to stand with one foot over the cliff at all times."

Like so many of her fellow actors, she knows she can count on God. "God does not give you the talent and then not provide you with the ability to carry it through. You have to firmly believe that and act as if it's true." This doesn't mean she's not afraid sometimes, but she says even Jesus experienced fear as he prayed in the garden the night before he laid down his life. "It's not that we're not supposed to be afraid. Fear can exist in the presence of faith, but you just have to act 'as if'"—as if everything will be all right.

That faith has landed her on Broadway in *Titanic*, national touring companies of *Jekyll and Hyde*, *Les Misérables*, *The Who's Tommy* and *Jesus Christ Superstar* and numerous Off-Broadway shows. She also shares the bandstand with some of the world's great jazz musicians in clubs in and around New York and has recorded her first CD, *Bertilla Baker*, with John Hicks on piano, Walter Booker on bass and Billy Hart on drums.

She keeps focused by singing in the choir at First Presbyterian Church in Brooklyn and The Riverside Church in Manhattan. Although she grew up Catholic in Watertown, New York, she lost interest in that tradition after the Second Vatican Council ended in 1965 and music standards plunged to what she calls "truly wretched." It is because liturgical music is important to her that she was able to connect so quickly with McElroy's choir. "Hearing this kind of music from a black Baptist tradition brought an intensity I had never experienced before. It just calls in the presence of the Holy Spirit, which is palpable, real, and intense."

And immediate. That presence was there the first day she walked in to rehearse with the choir. McElroy had separated the singers, listening to each section before putting them together. "When I heard all the voices it was such an awesome sound and feeling I couldn't believe I was there. I really believe God put me there and put that tape in Michael's hand. God arranges everything."

The message of the music has deepened and broadened her faith. "The poetry of the lyrics is so deep and so moving and inspiring it affects your entire being. You can't sing this music and not be changed by it." Which is why she puts in many hours of rehearsal and sings in the concerts for little or no pay. "It's such a blessing and a gift to me personally and artistically. It's the thing I'm proudest of having done musically in my life. I've worked the hardest on it and been paid the least, but the spiritual payoff reverberates back. God put me in the position of putting this message out. It's a source of contact between people and our God. We're all praying to the same God, and singing is absolutely prayer."

The power of the music is enhanced by McElroy's direction, Baker says. "Michael has the ears of life and he hears everything, the notes and the inflections. It's like decorating a hall for the Holy Spirit to come in. When the inspiration comes into the music it's nothing you can explain." And that power goes out to the audience. Baker says one song that really touches people is "Stand," with its message that after you've done all you can, then stand and watch for the Lord to come through. During one concert nearly everyone in the room was in tears, with audience members embracing each other. "Strangers were so moved by the message and the feeling of the Spirit, and I was so grateful to be part of it."

And that's how Baker lives her life—full of gratitude. "My main prayer is 'please God, increase my faith.' If he'll do that, everything else will be okay, and I know he will because he has. If you ask something that's in God's will you'll get it. My life is like the miracle of the loaves and fishes. Every day when it looks like there's absolutely no way, a way appears out of thin air. Not just occasionally, but frequently. That's why performing artists are the way we are. A lot seems to come out of thin air." So she sings, practices gratitude, and reads the Bible on a regular basis. And she prays. "I don't use formal prayers like I did when I was raised Catholic. Mostly I just talk and listen."

Talking and listening to God also works well for Kristin Chenoweth, who grew up Southern Baptist. "I don't do a lot of bowing my head before bed, but when I'm walking down the street I talk to God. I'll say, 'Dear Lord, that man doesn't have enough to eat.'" Most of her prayer is like this, sort of a conversation with God, although she would like to find more time to read scripture. "I want to spend more time with the word. That's what I grew up with, but a lot of things get in the way now."

Things getting in the way include theatre, television, concerts, special events and recording her own CD, *Let Yourself Go*. One method she uses for working in some scripture reading is to turn to the Psalm and Proverb for whatever day of the month it is, which means if it's the fifteenth of the month, she reads Psalm and Proverb 15. "I want to learn to memorize more because I believe it helps you. The Bible is here to help us. I don't know why people don't want to use it. I believe it's truly inspired by God, so I believe it."

For her, God is not a being to be afraid of, even when she makes mistakes. "He wants us to call on him. He's looking down, wanting us to rely on him. That's not exactly the Southern Baptist belief I grew up with, but it's how I believe now." She relies on that sense of God to see her through all the stresses of an acting career and the pressure of people's expectations, which seem to grow as one advances in the profession. "Like most actors, I have my insecurities. My prayer with the Lord every day is not to take things personally. I say, 'Okay, you gave me this gift. Help me not to doubt it.'"

It is because the profession is so full of doubt and rejection that many actors find strength in religion. "Performing artists and people in general need to connect with their core faith to express their joys and sorrows," says Rabbi David Baron, founder in 1992 of Temple Shalom for the Arts in Los Angeles. "There's a need to connect, to share with others." Filling that need is the Temple's mission: "To reconnect fellow Jews and all people seeking spiritual enlightenment with the beliefs and traditions of Judaism through the arts." Baron says his synagogue does this by bringing in artists from diverse backgrounds to create "new expressions of Jewish worship." Prayer at Temple Shalom for the Arts is articulated through dramatic readings done by actors in the congregation, original music composed for its services, dance, and the visual arts. "We're doing a blend of religion, music, art, and dance. That's our mission. That's what we're all about. We're a temple of the arts."

Although Baron had served conservative congregations before founding Temple Shalom for the Arts, his current congregation is unaffiliated with any major movement. "We take advice from everyone, but orders from no one but God," he says.

Over the years, services, which meet on the third Friday of each month at the Writers Guild Theater in Beverly Hills, had become so popular they were attracting close to a thousand people before Baron required worshipers to make reservations. The service is free and people may bring guests, but reservations help the staff prepare better for the worship and reception that follows. Now between five hundred and six hundred people attend, says Baron, who also performs weddings, bar mitzvahs, and bat mitzvahs throughout the year.

Choir members sing songs composed especially for them by a variety of musicians. Barry Gordon, a former president of the Screen Actors Guild and one of the Temple's two cantors, composed one of these, "Don't Let the Candle Die," for a Purim play. The song is about not allowing the light of faith to be extinguished even in the darkest of times. Gordon sings it with the other cantor, Ilysia Pierce, who appeared in *Beauty and the Beast* on Broadway and on tour. Music also is composed in response to certain world events, such as the 2001 terrorists attacks in the United States and Israel, for which "God's Will" was written. That song is one of eleven the choir released on its first CD, *Enlighten*, in the fall of 2002.

Songs and prayers in the services use Hebrew as well as English, and dramatic readings draw upon traditional Jewish themes of atonement, reconciliation, belief, and struggle. "A great piece of music or a reading beautifully done can touch people in a strong way," Baron says. Services are different every month and have included a fifty-voice black gospel choir for a Shared Heritage of Freedom evening, which had the two choirs jamming at the end.

High Holy Days services are held at the two-thousand-seat art deco Wilshire Theatre, also in Beverly Hills. Congregants use a special prayer book, *Sacred Moments*, created by the Temple, with prayers, meditations, and thirty-one prints of Marc Chagall. For regular monthly services another Temple-created prayer book, *Sacred Space*, is used. "These are wonderful gifts people offer," Baron says. "They can write prayers. It's not just the usual ways of contributing financially. People volunteer in artistic ways." This includes the contribution of a set designer who created a model of the Western Wall, the holiest site in Judaism, "to connect Jews of all denominations."

The Temple's efforts to connect Jews and to reach out to an even larger community have gone far beyond its physical space in California. In 1999 it coproduced for the History Channel a forty-five-minute documentary, *Diplomats for the Damned*, the story of four diplomats serving in German-occupied countries during World War II who risked their careers and possibly their lives to rescue Jews and others marked for death by the Nazis. The Temple has sent more than five thousand of these videos, along with teachers' guides, all over the United States. It also has connected to Jews in seven major cities in the United States and Canada with televised Yom Kippur services to "bring the synagogue to those who cannot come to the synagogue."

"I was always interested in reaching more people," Baron says. "I came out of mainstream conservative congregations that weren't getting the message out. If you're only preaching to ten people, you're not getting the message out. My goal was to maximize attendance, with relevancy and meaning, by bringing in artistic expression so people who were not coming to temple would come. Now I'm reaching a constituency that was always there, but didn't feel pulled to come. The arts bring people across the threshold."

The synagogue's approach works because it responds to the needs of the time, Baron says. "The Hebrew word for prayer means to turn inward. We live in an age of so many distractions. It's very hard to have the quiet necessary to turn inward. It's not something we can do instantly, so we look for whatever means we can use to prepare and induce us into prayer and turning inward. There are so many beeping and ringing devices. Whatever we can do as preparation for prayer is to our advantage."

For the Rev. George Drance, S.J., prayer is a way of dealing with the ancient human need to find more than we experience on the surface of life. "The two ways through history that we've embodied that struggle are through religious expression and theatrical expression." As a Jesuit priest, actor, and acting instructor at Fordham University, Drance is familiar with both of those ways. "I pray before every performance, sometimes by myself and sometimes the group I am with will ask me to lead them. I dedicate my performance to God and try to focus on emptying myself so the Spirit can find a clear channel."

The two prayers he favors are from the Divine Liturgy of St. John Chrysostom: "We who mystically represent the Cherubim/and sing the thrice-holy hymn to the life-giving Trinity,/let us lay aside all earthly cares/that we may welcome the King of all escorted by unseen hosts" and "Oh Heavenly King, Consoler, Spirit of Truth,/present in all places and filling all things/the Treasury of Spirit, and the giver of Life,/Come! Oh Good One, and dwell in us,/cleanse us from all ill, and save our souls."

His prayers as a priest include celebration of the Eucharist as often as possible; intercessory prayers for others; the Divine Office, which he calls "part of my personal prayer which unites me to the church"; and spontaneous prayers throughout the day. "I don't think I would be able to be a priest without personal prayer. Prayer is an integral part of my life as a priest, for others and myself as well."

He sees a link in his roles as priest and actor, one that was central to two famous leaders in those callings—Jesuit founder St. Ignatius Loyola and founder of The Method school of acting, Konstantin Stanislavsky, both of whom placed emphasis on developing use of the senses. "God made things that impact our senses. For Ignatius, this was one of the ways God reveals himself to us. Finding God in all things made his prayer come alive." Employing the senses could be used to deepen contemplation by "vividly impacting" scripture study, he says, while developing one's power of observation heightens awareness of the spirit working in everyday life.

In the case of Stanislavsky, what was really important was the physical action, the "commingling of action and intention," says Drance who holds a master of fine arts degree in acting from Columbia University and is co-author of the book *Ritual Plays*. "To be that focused and involved, you have to be here and now, in the moment. Being in the present moment is essential in both theatre and prayer. The present moment is the moment of revelation. Nothing makes us more in the moment than concentrating upon what actually is in front of us. The way things enter our consciousness is through our senses."

Using observation helps the actor to create a life situation in concentrated form in a way we miss in our daily experience because we filter out much that could threaten our psychological survival, says Drance, who has performed and directed in more than fifteen countries on five continents, as well as worked with La MaMa Experimental Theatre Club of New York, the American Repertory Theater, and ImprovBoston. He says it is the artist's job to show the intensity in manageable doses, to give people a sense of God's grace working in their lives. Concentrated observation leads both actors and people on the spiritual journey past the filters to an experience of awe. This awe can lead to both a shared theatrical experience and gratitude in prayer.

Drance has found a way to enhance his prayer and acting lives by using Stanislavsky's emphasis on developing observation skills, and he encourages his students in this as well. The observation that is needed is not just of others—the way they talk or move—but also of one's self on the interior level where emotions live. "Through observation of behavior we achieve what is a hip theatre word now, 'specificity.' The more I observe, the more particulars I have to choose from. The more I have to choose from, the more it will make my choices specific." This attunes him to a deeper emotional level from which to draw, but it also is a good spiritual tool. "When people observe themselves, they often neglect the spiritual observation. We tend to observe behavior, but sometimes we're afraid to observe our emotional state." By exploring our emotional lives, we can see what triggers our behavior. "Those moments of heightened emotion point to a spiritual movement within ourselves, a movement to God or away from God."

Which is why this technique, known as Examination of Conscience or Consciousness, is part of Jesuit training. It involves spending time every evening—and afternoon, if possible—to reflect on the day, looking at where one has been open to God's presence or where one might have shut out that presence, with a special emphasis on relationships. Drance advises his acting students to follow this approach.

"I first teach this practice as a good way to be aware of our personal patterns, to remember moments of heightened emotion throughout the day." He wants students to understand what makes them want to scream on the subway or dance in the park. "These point to something happening in us emotionally or spiritually. We can trace a line backward to find the source of that emotion." Wanting to scream on the subway can be traced to being late and feeling stressed, which can be traced to hitting the snooze button once too often. The ensuing irritability and stress can affect relationships throughout the day. St. Ignatius called this habit of paying attention to what's going on in one's mind "the discernment of spirits."

"By tracing things backward I can see for myself what makes me happy and what makes me sad. In becoming aware of our patterns we are aware of how free or unfree we are before God. If I have the habit of becoming angry I could say, 'Oh, that's just who I am' or see the possibility of growing in patience. Do I lash out in panicky self-defense, or do I allow myself to observe myself along the way? When I observe a pattern repeating itself, I can remember my God-given freedom to go against it rather than endlessly repeating the pattern. I can see where something is going and I can pray for patience." Awareness, when practiced, becomes a habit, he says.

Looking back in this way will increase one's awareness that God is present with one throughout the day, Drance says. "When I observe moments of joy or compassion I affirm that God is a part of my life and I acknowledge how God works for me in my life. This leads me to gratitude, and gratitude and awe are the most satisfying places to be in prayer."

He is again served in both areas of his life. "Prayer gives people in general and actors in particular a sense of wider possibilities." And as a priest, it is essential. "Catholicism is, for those of us who are Catholic, the way of life established by God in the person of Christ incarnate, crucified, resurrected, and present in his Spirit. To participate in that mystery of God's love I have to be attuned to that mystery. Prayer is the way in which I attune myself."

Self-Knowledge

O Lord, my heart is not lifted up,
my eyes are not raised too high;
I do not occupy myself with things
too great and too marvelous for me.
~PSALM 131:1

Life's not worth a damn 'til you can say,
"Hey, world, I am what I am."
~JERRY HERMAN, *La Cage aux Folles*

SELF-KNOWLEDGE, another crucial element in an actor's life, is necessary for any spiritual journey. Proverbs 4:7 says: "The beginning of wisdom is this: Get wisdom, and whatever else you get, get insight." The prophet Sirach tells us: "Like clay in the hands of a potter, to be molded according to his pleasure, so are people in the hands of their Creator, to be assigned by him their function." The trick is knowing one's self well enough to discern this function. It takes work for all of us, but actors have special challenges. They play so many roles onstage they face the danger of losing themselves. They need to develop a spiritual centering to avoid being taken over by a

character, as well as all the hype that often surrounds their performances and their personal lives.

But then, this is the key for all of us, to know who we are and live
out of that knowledge. As Margaret says to her sister, Helen, in E. M.
Forster's book *Howard's End*: "All over the world men and women are
worrying because they cannot develop as they are supposed to
develop. . . . Don't fret yourself, Helen. Develop what you have."

It's hard, though, to develop one's self in a world filled with
rejection and criticism, which all of us face at some point, though
rarely at the frequency with which actors must cope. Knowing who
we are keeps us from doubting ourselves. As Lucio says in *Measure for
Measure*: "Our doubts are traitors / And make us lose the good we oft
might win, / By fearing to attempt." We then are in danger of becoming somebody else's creation. Edward Young, an eighteenth-century
British poet, knew this when he said: "We're born originals and
die copies."

But we don't have to. Our originality comes from our discovery of
who we are created and called to be. "I have no problem growing
older," Vanessa Williams says. "With age I have more power, more
control, and less anxiety."

While more power may have come with age, Williams has had a
remarkable self-knowledge since childhood. She attributes her strong
sense of self to her parents, music teachers who encouraged Williams
and her younger brother, Christopher, to do things for themselves,
helping them to build confidence as they took on—and mastered—
new tasks. "I always had an identity which was strong. My parents
made me independent at an early age. They applauded and encouraged my intelligence. They exposed me to a lot so I wasn't isolated."

And she follows their example with her four children. "I want
my kids to be self-sufficient. They'll function better in life. Let them

do things for themselves as young as one or two instead of [me] doing everything for them. That's helped in my own child-rearing."

Williams's parents could have had no way of predicting just how much she was going to need her self-knowledge. After she was born on March 18, 1963, her parents sent birth announcements reading: "Here She Is, Miss America!" And in twenty years that's just what she would be, although being a beauty queen was not part of her plan. Her yearbook caption from Horace Greeley High School in Chappaqua, New York, declared: "I'll see you on Broadway." But in her junior year at Syracuse University while pursuing a degree in musical theatre, she won the local pageant, which she had entered to earn money for books and possibly supplement her scholarship. After she was crowned Miss Greater Syracuse, it was on to the state pageant and then, as Miss New York, to Atlantic City where on September 17, 1983, she was crowned the first black Miss America. Jubilant students back at Syracuse University filled the streets, shouting out her name.

"Objectively I knew I was intelligent enough and talented enough to be Miss America, but it wasn't my goal," she says.

Her reign tested all those inner strengths she had been building since childhood. In the black community she was loved as a role model by some and criticized as being too light-skinned by others. Then there was the Ku Klux Klan with its stream of hate letters. At one stop in Alabama she needed an armed guard posted twenty-four hours a day outside her motel room door. She felt with that security she was safe, but she worried about her family back home because they had received threats as well.

This was a lot for a twenty-year-old to cope with, but Williams was no ordinary twenty-year-old. She had first encountered racism growing up in Millwood, a predominantly white suburb forty miles northeast of New York City. When she was in third grade she heard the word *nigger* for the first time. "I knew I was different in my school system," she says. In high school, where she was one of only a few black girls, a white friend of hers was called "nigger-lover." Nothing she had experienced, though, equaled the Klan hatred. She drew upon the inner reserves her parents had built in her. "I had a great foundation. Certainly it hurt my feelings, and there were days I wanted to give it up."

Eventually she did give it up, just seven weeks before her reign would have ended. Racism wasn't the reason, though. On Friday, July 13, 1984, an anonymous caller warned that nude photos she had posed for at nineteen, when she was assured they were for artistic purposes and in which she would never be identified, would appear in the September issue of *Penthouse* magazine. For one week she could barely eat or sleep, wondering how bad the photos were, but still having to go on with appearances, smiling her Miss America smile. When the news did break, reaction was strong. *Penthouse* publisher Bob Guccione received more than two hundred death threats by phone or mail, and the magazine's offices had to be vacated for two hours because of a bomb threat. Her family rallied to her side, and her father received a call from the Rev. Jesse Jackson telling her to hold her head high. Her hometown, which had already demonstrated its pride in her with a road sign reading: "You Are Now Entering Millwood, Home of Vanessa Williams, Miss America, 1984," rose to her defense, with teenagers organizing a Victory for Vanessa rally that paraded past her house. She and her family discussed whether she should fight to hold on to her crown or resign. On July 23, with her characteristic poise firmly intact, she held a press conference to announce her decision—she was resigning to get on with her career.

And get on with it she did.

Taking a detour from her Broadway goal, she launched a recording career in 1988 with her first album, *The Right Stuff*, which went gold and earned her first three Grammy Award nominations. Her multimillion-selling follow-up, *The Comfort Zone*, and third album, *The Sweetest Days*, each yielded multiple hits and Grammy nominations. Her hit single "Colors of the Wind" from Disney's *Pocahontas* won the Academy Award, Golden Globe, and Grammy for Best Song in a Motion Picture.

But she never lost sight of her original ambition—Broadway. She had been waiting a long time, since she was eleven and her parents took her to the Broadway musical *The Wiz*, starring Stephanie Mills, and she knew that's what she wanted for her life. Her wait ended in 1994 after she was cast as the lead in *The Kiss of the Spider Woman*, taking over for Chita Rivera, who had won a Tony Award for the role. Lines formed at the theatre box office within weeks, with Williams playing to standing-room-only houses; the show, which had had 70 percent attendance, leapt to 100 percent. Her engagement was supposed to last three months, but Williams extended it to six, then nine, leaving only because she had to promote an album overseas.

"I never doubted it would happen. I knew I could sing, dance, and act. If I wasn't talented I don't think my parents would have encouraged me and given me the tools. I never sat down and tried to decipher why. I just knew I'd get there eventually."

And when she did, it was everything she could have wanted. "That first opening night was a collective dream. All my friends from Syracuse were there and my high school friends. It was thrilling. There was nothing like it. I will cherish that night."

Making it even better, critics praised her performance. In his July 31, 1994, *New York Times* review, Vincent Canby wrote: "She's not a performer who holds back. She's throwing everything she has into this performance, which pays off with the audience." He acknowledged Rivera was a hard act to follow, but that Williams "appears to have both the intelligence and the intuition that separate merely competent performers from those who are first rate and more."

Her talent brought her the praise, but her deep-seated self-confidence was a contributing factor. "When you're replacing someone larger than life like Chita, you have to make it your own," she says. "Some people might not have taken the part because they would feel they would always be compared to Chita." She had the same attitude in 2002 for the Broadway revival of *Into the Woods* and her role as The Witch, which Bernadette Peters originated in 1987. "That's how I approached this one, too. Bernadette was wonderful, but I knew what I would bring would be different and equally as interesting." Which is just what director James Lapine had in mind. "We sort of wanted to go against the grain," he said in a February 24, 2002, *New York Times* interview. "We needed somebody with an edge. It's kind of a wild card part. It's a star part. We needed someone to command the stage."

Taking command is something Williams knew how to do. In an August 1994 *Essence* interview, Radu, her personal trainer, summed it up this way: "There may be other people out there who have it, but they're afraid of becoming the best. It's like having the strength and potential and then not developing it." Williams, he said, "is not afraid of her strength."

Looking back on her journey to Broadway, she remarked to one of her college acting teachers about the irony that she, who was such a determined student of musical theatre, should be first famous for being a beauty queen. "The fact is that I'm now on Broadway doing what I wanted to do twenty years ago. It would have been quicker and I would have been taken more seriously quicker if I hadn't been Miss America. Obviously that was my path. It all happened for a reason."

Now she is offered far more work in a variety of fields than she can take on, and she once again relies on her self-knowledge. "I decide purely on gut reaction what I want to do and what challenges me and has integrity. Twenty years ago I wanted to be seen and I needed money and wanted to build my career. Now I feel it in my soul. If I read a script, can I imagine and picture myself in this particular role? It's the same with music. I might think it's a beautiful song, but it's not me."

She employed this strategy in 1999 when given the script for *Monster's Ball*. She turned down the part that won Halle Berry an Academy Award in 2002 and the distinction of being the first black woman to win a Best Actress Oscar. Williams second-guessed herself at first when Oscar talk around the movie began, but she knew she had had her reasons for turning down the part. "In my heart I knew I could act the role and show a side of me people had never seen, but I didn't feel comfortable with it. There were problems with the character and story. I went with my gut."

Because she trusts herself, she makes it a policy not to read articles written about her. "They're always just one person's perception," she says, adding that often they are downright lies. She also has learned not to be defensive when people express surprise, which they often do, at her various abilities. "With everything I've accomplished I've heard comments like, 'I didn't know she could do that.' Over the years, as opposed to when I was in my twenties, I've learned to embrace it. People have low expectations, unfortunately. In this industry, there's so much labeling. People's first impression of me was as a beauty queen, then a recording artist, now a Broadway star. I'm lucky to be multifaceted. I can sing, dance, do television. Instead of being angry, now I say graciously, 'Thank you.'"

She has been in training a long time to get to that point. "My mother said, 'You'll have to do better at everything just to be considered equal.' That's how I lived my life and how I continue to live my life."

For Edward Herrmann, self-discovery has come through intense reading, discussion, and seeking on his spiritual journey. Raised Unitarian in Grosse Point, Michigan, he found that practice lacked regularity, dependent on inspiration and enthusiasm, which can wax and wane. "No enthusiasm is so great that it can keep you going," he says.

While exploring Eastern religions, he was drawn to Buddhism and followed a guru. Despite the useful techniques he learned for centering, he calls this experience "a near catastrophe." The guru later hanged himself, but "I was out of it by then."

It was Catholicism that finally hooked him.

"When I was a child in the fifties, the Catholic children were insufferable," he says of their insistence that they belonged to The One True Church. But now he sees it differently. "It's true. The fullness is revealed here. Catholicism is the most rigorous of all the traditions."

In that rigor he has found comfort in the familiarity of set prayers and in the transcendence of the Mass. "Gradually I find the formality of the old liturgical prayers appeals to me." He reads daily from an 1880s version of *The Following of Christ*, a prayer book written by Thomas Á Kempis, a fifteenth-century ascetical writer. It includes traditional morning and evening prayers, reflections on St. Thomas, what it means to follow Christ, and how one can go about it. "It doesn't lose itself in social commentary. It goes right to the heart of things." Herrmann found the prayer book in his parents' desk drawer. It had belonged to a distant relative who was a nun. Since it had four-leaf clovers in it, Herrmann had it re-bound with a shamrock on the cover and now carries it with him on acting jobs. He likes the morning and evening prayers and the litanies to the Blessed Virgin—"each one is a meditation of its own." In addition to saying set prayers, he attends Sunday Mass at St. Mary's Church in Lakeville, Connecticut. Although his wife is a Mormon—"we have some amusing debates about the afterlife"—their daughter was baptized Catholic.

Spending time as a pilgrim on the spiritual journey has brought him to Catholicism, but he still maintains respect for other faiths. "Buddhism is the most attractive besides Christianity because it is the most useful, the most benign. But Christianity is the most complex and by far the richest and greatest. There's nothing remotely like it in its complexity and power." He contrasts the difference in Eastern religions and Christianity as the former placing emphasis on people lifting themselves out of the world, while Christianity teaches "you can't abandon the world, no matter how much you want to."

While he has found Catholicism to be the way for him, he finds fault with the way it has played out in the decades following the end of the Second Vatican Council in 1965. "We judge ourselves by the standards of the day rather than the other way around. The meaning of Christianity is entirely different from a relief organization. We're here to save souls." He believes some doors were opened after Vatican II, but says more harm was done. One of the most problematic reforms he sees was changing the language of the Mass into the vernacular from Latin, which allowed one to participate in Mass anywhere in the world. "There's no cohesive language. The loss of liturgical regularity is a catastrophe."

He attributes his strong opinions to his being a convert. "Coming from the Unitarian Church I may be overemphasizing to make a point. Unitarians are forced to accept any idea that comes down the pike because they're afraid they won't be current. There's no theology, no dogma, no law. Every single Sunday they're trying to define what Unitarian is. It's filled with angry people with an ax to grind, former Catholics and Jews and people from other religions."

His decision to become a Catholic didn't sit well with his mother, a liberal Democrat and former Planned Parenthood president. Her father had been a Catholic and she didn't have much use for him. "It was a blow to her when I went Catholic. I told her 'Watch what I do, not what I say.'"

Not only has he changed his views on religion over the years, but his understanding of the way one should live one's life has changed as well. "In the sixties and seventies when sex was free and there was no disease, we thought it was great. We could sleep with anyone and we did. It's a lie. The fact that we did it didn't make it true. It's not enlightening and helpful. We didn't look for connections, for relationships. It was a bogus rainbow-hair life."

He is also critical of much of the experimental theatre he participated in then for its emphasis on pushing a message. "People want a release from their workaday worlds. That's what the arts are for, an experience. I'm nervous about artists, so-called artists, who use the arts for political reasons. Now you're ramming something down people's throats, to remind the audience you have an agenda. It destroys the sense of a Forest in Arden. People want to leave themselves so they can experience something transcendent."

He compares that transcendence to the celebration of the Mass. "The Mass is experiential. It's not fundamentally rational. We believe in the Real Presence [of Christ in the Eucharist] and our Protestant and Jewish friends think we're crazy; but they do the same thing when they go to the opera. It's all about experiencing something."

A similar connection can be made between acting in theatre and praying, he says. "Being onstage, it's hard with eight shows a week to keep it fresh. It becomes, on another level, being able to manipulate the situation and entertain the audience night after night. It's different from the spark. Noël Coward said maybe you can get the spark three out of the eight times. Mostly it's just remember your lines and don't bump into the furniture."

Actors carry on with the "sensory memory" they develop after four or five weeks of rehearsal, just as people on the spiritual journey learn to move on. "It's like being dry in prayer. You go to prayer thinking you can't do it, but you go through the motions. That's why I like set prayer. I find the regularity of it refreshing."

In discovering his new faith, Herrmann has found a third connection between theatre and religion—what he calls the Catholicism of Shakespeare's plays. "All his plays are about one thing—grace—either received or rejected on some level. That's pure medieval Catholicism."

Whether acting in a Shakespeare play or other theatrical entertainment, Herrmann says actors help audiences fulfill a universal need. "They offer a kind of safety zone where someone can go and play and use muscles they don't in the marketplace. We don't play enough. We take it out in sports, or affairs, or drinking, but the arts allow us to experience something together as a community. They lift people out of themselves so they can find themselves."

In finding ourselves, we tap into the inner strength to sustain our God-given creative gifts. Stage, TV, and film actor Ann Dowd learned this when she looked for a way to overcome her "regular history with stage fright."

"I thought, 'I really don't have to live with this. I love being an actress. I consider it one of the greatest gifts in my life. I don't have to accept this. I could let it go if I understood it.'"

Her stage fright was hard to understand because, although she had it most of the time, she didn't have it all of the time. It wasn't there in 1993 when she played Prossy in *Candida*, her first Broadway performance, a time of great excitement—and anxiety—for most actors. "Something remarkable happened," she says. "I was utterly calm and energized. I had no fear. I had never experienced that in my life, let alone onstage." What did the trick was imagining that the stage was a shelf extending into the audience, which made her feel a oneness, that she and the audience were the same.

But when it came time for her second Broadway role, that of Tamara in *Taking Sides* in 1996, the stage fright returned with a vengeance. "It's so draining. It's about fear and it keeps you from being present because you're too busy fighting off something. When you are present, everything is possible. You're not afraid because you know everything you need is there."

That's what she knows now, but at the time she was "desperate" to find a way to overcome her fear. She got a book on meditation and spent twenty minutes meditating every day, which did more than just calm her. "Life was amazing. I felt like I was at a carnival. I couldn't get over the joy of it." She went to see the movie *The English Patient* and "felt like I had never been to the movies before."

She learned her life could be much fuller if she slowed down her thoughts and expectations for quick solutions, took deep breaths, and stayed in the present moment. Then, before she had a chance to keep this awareness working against her stage fright, she was cast in 1997 as Sister Maureen in the ABC-TV series *Nothing Sacred* and she no longer had to deal with the anxieties of live theatre. "I loved the experience, the people, and the role. Time spent with a character in different circumstances is tremendously liberating. You're not re-creating the same character eight times a week like in theatre. Once I know the character, I'm not distracted in what I'm doing." Her secure feeling was enhanced by working with the Rev. Bill Cain, S.J., the series' creator and one of its writers, and line editor Cyrus Yavneh. "They kept an open door. I felt I could express my opinion and be heard."

But although the series, about an urban Roman Catholic parish and the issues it faced, was critically praised, it had low ratings. Because it dealt with topics like priest celibacy, the ordination of women, abortion, and pedophilia, it came under attack by conservative groups, most notably the Catholic League for Religious and Civil Rights. Sponsors shied away and the series was canceled before the end of the first season.

Knowing she would most likely be heading back into theatre work and afraid the stage fright would return, Dowd sought the help of a healer in California. As soon as Dowd walked into the room, the healer, who knew nothing about her, mentioned the "significant amount of fear you're carrying around." As Dowd shared her frustration over the recurring problem, the healer began having conversations with Dowd's "spirits," which only the healer could hear. She told Dowd to stay in her body and helped her see she had been so busy striving to manage her experience that she had not been aware of the help she had within. "My fear was because I was trying so hard to get control I was blocking everything else out. Whatever spirits or aid I had, I couldn't receive it or hear it because I was so busy trying to keep things in control."

That habit of trying to control things was still at work as she tried to push forward, until her spirits told her to slow down and practice awareness. "They said, 'It's not a race. There's no magic potion.'"

Deciding to test this notion of inner help, she called upon it before her next audition. "I said, 'I want to experience this character when I go in the room.'" And she did. "I was shocked at what happened, the subtle pieces of information that came to me. The healer had said if you listen, you have a lot of help coming your way."

This has changed her perspective on the audition process. "You have tremendous power as an actor, even in an audition. That role is yours for those five minutes. Behave as though it's yours. If you're present with that character for that time, you'll walk out feeling good."

Besides being instructed to listen to her inner voices, Dowd learned from her healer to practice yoga twice a week. Combining this with meditation has been a big help. "I now have an awareness that acting is fun, it is pleasurable. I have an awareness that this is okay. I try to take the reverence out of it . . . this is the ground, this is the wall, this is the audience."

And it worked when she starred in *An Immaculate Misconception* Off-Broadway in the fall of 2001. Although in the opening scene she was in bed onstage, often with her breasts exposed, she wasn't afraid, even though in the small theatre the audience was quite close. She caught the eye of a woman in a front row one night and realized her work toward self-knowledge had paid off. "I thought, 'That's just a person. You're human and they're human and there's nothing to be afraid of here.'" By staying in the present moment, she overcomes her fear. "That's the only place that real creativity comes from. Everything else is from memory. It's the most powerful way to communicate."

This way of attaining self-knowledge is different from what she was taught growing up Roman Catholic in Springfield, Massachusetts, where she went to Mass with her family and attended the Ursuline Academy. Her grandmother had "rock-solid faith" and two of her aunts are nuns, but she never felt moved by Catholicism. "I was surrounded by that, but I never really caught on to the Church. There were very few priests who moved me. I was never attracted to the Church in terms of informing my life." In her experience of Catholicism, the joy was left out, with emphasis placed too much on suffering and repentance. "I'm very spiritual now. It's real, being present and in real time. It's also joyful and meaningful. I realize I have a great life."

She does respect the sense of community she finds when she visits her aunts and likes the way the other sisters really listen to her and her two children. She also is influenced by another nun, the fictional one she played on *Nothing Sacred*. Sister Maureen wanted to be a priest in the Catholic Church, which doesn't ordain women. "She's practical and funny and Irish, which is to say she naturally looked at things with humor and some level of wit. I loved her knowledge that she had a rightful place in the Church, on the altar with everyone else. She had tremendous confidence. I loved that about her. She knew her place in the world. She was very sensible. When I'm feeling focused and in myself, I think of her."

Other actors talk about learning from characters they play and how they use that knowledge to better perform their roles and enrich their own lives. "When I have spurts of growth personally, they make my character better," actor and producer Amanda Blair Ellis says. "What I learn about a character makes me stronger. They feed each other." The art of becoming someone else onstage is, therefore, essential for Ellis in her own journey of self-discovery. "The process of exploring somebody else allows me to step outside myself and try things I wouldn't necessarily do in my own life. On the one hand, I pull from myself to make the character and on the other, the character pulls from me. I've become more self-assured by trying new things as an actor."

She thinks because actors are forced to explore a range of emotions on a regular basis, they can attain a heightened self-knowledge.

"Actors are always in the process of deepening their craft and deepening themselves as human beings. Many times we delve much deeper than people do in their daily lives."

The greatest challenge to staying grounded, she says, is audition season, when actors hold themselves out to be judged, sometimes more than once in a day, facing rejection time and again. She relies heavily on journal writing to keep her centered. "It's a roller coaster of emotions, a constant self-evaluation process."

The self-knowledge they acquire, though, helps actors lead others into a self-evaluation process of their own. "Storytelling is an important part of humanity. Theatre has grown out of that storytelling tradition. It's a chance for us to take a look at ourselves. When an audience comes into a theatre they take a journey and come out on a different side. The journey stretches the audience to become better themselves and more aware of different people and experiences." This doesn't have to be a major catharsis. "It could just be letting go of your own worries and troubles for a while and sharing a good experience with a friend."

Cantor Heather Tamar Feffer says attaining self-knowledge is a central aim of Jewish prayer. In the *amidah*, a silent standing prayer that is part of the morning ritual, one asks God for wisdom and understanding. "Self-knowledge is inherent in Jewish prayer every day," Feffer says. "Not only self-knowledge, but wisdom to know what to do with what you have. For me, Jewish prayer is about reflection." It is turning to God, the giver of knowledge, every morning with the words "You graciously endow people with knowledge and teach insight to us. Endow us graciously from yourself with wisdom, insight, and knowledge."

Feffer, a former Protestant who converted to Judaism in 1990, holds a graduate degree from New York University's division of performance studies. Self-knowledge is essential to her whether she is leading a congregation in song or singing her extensive Yiddish repertoire before an audience. "When I knew who I was, that's when I could be before an audience in the theatre or a congregation."

Self-knowledge is the key that opens doors, she says. Trying to maintain a religious practice without it amounts to little more than following a crowd. "Self-knowledge is knowing what you're meant to be in life. It's more than 'I have brown hair and blue eyes.' It's not about appearance. It's internal knowledge." And it's up to each person to uncover it. "Everyone is on a special path. When we stray, problems arise. We don't see them until we stop. Knowledge is when to stop and see what we need to explore in our lives."

Continually stopping to reflect is the way to achieve self-knowledge, she says, and self-knowledge leads to self-worth. "It's knowing that if our lives were just a wheel, like the expression 'same old same old,' then we're not knowing ourselves. We're stuck in a one-way cycle. Self-knowledge is knowing that you're worthy to be standing on this earth and what you're meant to do and meant to be." This, in turn, benefits society. "If we each know what we're meant to be, we're not looking at someone else and saying, 'I want to be you.' You know your own contribution and this helps against jealousy and other things that break down society."

The reflectiveness of Jewish prayer helps one gain self-knowledge, Feffer says. "You seek and desire something better than you have on earth today. It's not about going to church or synagogue communally, although that can help; you go inward where you can sit down and decide where you should be."

But first one has to step back from the hectic pace of everyday life. "Once I stop, that's the real time I can say who I am and why I'm here. I can see things that are not good and ask whether I have the courage to change them. What's important is being able to allow yourself time to stop." Which is why if Feffer could use only one word in advising people how to gain self-knowledge, it would be "stop." She's been stopping and questioning since at least her teen years, which is when she "felt powerfully" there was "something Jewish in me." Her mother was a member of the United Church of Christ and her father a Methodist; she worshiped with both traditions growing up in Milwaukee. But while she was a seventeen-year-old student at Northwestern University's National High School Institute, she was repeatedly thought to be Jewish and she began to feel pulled toward Judaism. When she was nineteen and in London, she saw the play *Ghetto*, about performing artists in the Vilna ghetto. "I had this profound transformation experience that this is what I was supposed to be."

Her conversion led her to Hebrew Union College–Jewish Institute of Religion where she studied in Jerusalem and New York City, earning a master's degree in sacred music and cantorial investiture. Her thesis, which picked up on the theatre degree she earned from the University of Iowa in Iowa City, was "From Second Avenue to the Synagogue: The Vital Connection between Theatre and Prayer," looking at an era when cantors were also regular performers on the stages of Second Avenue theatres in New York.

As a cantorial student she was intrigued with the question of how a prayer leader can lead the congregation and pray at the same time. She saw a connection between the desire to teach presence in both actors and prayer leaders and realized the prayer leader had to move deeply into prayer and not just be concerned with performance. "During the process of becoming a cantor, I found my theatre training a vital component to be present when prayer-leading others and praying to 'other.' Many, if not most, of all my cantorial and rabbinic classmates had both difficulties in connecting their own 'praying' to others while at the same time praying themselves. If you're not in the moment connecting with something other, then it's bad theatre."

Her exploration of this idea grew into a panel presentation given to a gathering of theatre academics in 2000 in Washington, D.C., entitled "Knowing Thyself: Spiritual Identity and the Possession of Performance." The panel considered the connection between how actors find their performance identities and how prayer leaders find their sense of presence when leading a congregation.

In the fall of 2002 she planned to draw upon her theatre background again in Jerusalem where she was being sent by Hebrew Union College for two years to teach rabbis and cantors how they could better teach prayer. She believes the prayer leader must be transformed to begin to know how to inspire and transform others. "Like any role, it's easy to be a stereotypical rabbi or cantor. You have to find out what kind of prayer leader you are and to know how to balance with other people's talents to form a network of creators." Feffer wants to introduce rabbis and cantors to the idea of ensemble theatre, in which no actor is the star and all perform equal parts.

"It's all about trying to understand yourself and how you react to human relationships, relate to God and yourself." Self-knowledge again comes into play. "Part of self-knowledge is knowing how to connect between your mind, your body, and your soul. In morning prayer there's a line that says, 'Thank you, God, for straightening the bent.' In theatre training, that's using posture, breathing, feet in place to connect to the world we live in. You have an awareness of being in the moment, of connecting to something unknown and another human being at the same time. You give up your self-consciousness by first having consciousness. Then you can get out of yourself and into another, whether human or 'other.'" The ability to do that involves stopping to become aware—on a regular basis. "Know what you need for your self-growth. Once you do, everything else will fall into place."

The Rev. Mitties DeChamplain says the quest for self-knowledge is "a lifelong coming to grips with who we really are as people created by God in a particular way." An Episcopal priest and homiletics professor at Manhattan's General Theological Seminary, she quotes from the

New Testament's Acts of the Apostles: "Lord, in you we live and move and have our being." For her, self-knowledge is inseparable from knowledge of God. "Coming to terms with who we are is done more truly in some kind of ongoing journey of faith, finding the self as spirit."

We lose touch with our true selves when we live out of other people's expectations rather than our own self-awareness, she says. "We're all made so fearfully and wonderfully, but societies induce conformity. So many people get dispirited because they get cut off from communities of people who care and encourage them to use their gifts."

This can be especially true in show business. DeChamplain quotes from the song "I Hope I Get It" in *A Chorus Line*: "Who am I anyway? Am I my resumé? . . . What does he want from me? What should I try to be?" "That's as far away from self-knowledge as a person can get. Our need for affirmation and approval makes us step outside the boundaries of our true selves."

People often lose sight of their gifts because they've "been called into being by negative voices." Those negative voices can break a person's spirit, causing them to lose touch with what enlivens them, what gives them pleasure. "There's deep satisfaction in your doing what you're meant to do. The ones who don't give up on that are the ones who thrive because we're all meant to do something."

This can be difficult because the soul-destroying criticism starts early, with parents who think they have to break a child's spirit and educational systems that are often based on negativity. "The world focuses on limitations."

DeChamplain says she was moved by the film *Spirit*, about a wild mustang captured by the cavalry, which fenced it in to tame it. "They couldn't because it wasn't made for that. It was made to run free, not be in a stable with a bit in its mouth. The people who have thrived are the ones who never lost the spirit."

The more we know God, the more likely we will be able to discern our true selves and our true purpose. "Freedom of choice is at the heart of being made in the image of God, to make good your own essence. But you have to find out what that is. When we're not happy doing what we're doing, our true self is suffering." She quotes St. Augustine: "O Lord, you have made us for yourself and our hearts are restless until they rest in thee." This is why the Episcopal Church places such emphasis on spiritual direction, she says. "Look at the events of your life with what the Spirit might be saying to you. Everyone has a voice inside calling them. The more self-aware we are, the more we can listen to the voice, but we have to be gutsy to follow the voice and trust we have an instinctive ability to choose because we're made in the image of God."

Another Broadway line comes to her to illustrate the point— "to love another person is to see the face of God," from the final song in *Les Misérables*. "I'm enough into the religious tradition of the Church to know I can't become self without becoming self in God. I'm free to bear the beauty of the divine in the way I do."

When we fail to pursue our destiny, we can end up in unfulfilling jobs. DeChamplain cites a third Broadway example, Leo Bloom in *The Producers*. "Leo has to earn a living, but he's stuck in a job with no satisfaction because it's not his vocation." His fellow accountants sing about being "very, very, very, very, very, very, very unhappy." Leo, who also is miserable, sings about what he really wants, quietly at first, then with gusto when he reveals his heart's longing. "I have a secret desire/hiding deep in my soul./It sets my heart afire/to see me in this role./I wanna be a producer/with a hit show on Broadway./I wanna be a producer,/lunch at Sardi's every day./I wanna be a producer,/sport a top hat and a cane./I wanna be a producer/and drive those chorus girls insane."

Finding theology in musical theatre comes naturally for DeChamplain, and not just because she loves going to the theatre. She is from a family of show people—her father was a casting director, her mother worked in a community playhouse and her brother is an actor. And in 2002 and 2003 she served as the presiding priest at St. Clement's Episcopal Church, which is no ordinary church. In a marriage that could possibly be consummated only in New York's theatre district, St. Clement's is at the same time a fully functioning Episcopal parish and a well-established Off-Broadway theatre.

Dramas performed in churches are not unusual. Many parishes use their halls for theatrical productions; others offer their sanctuaries with the stipulation that sets be cleared away before Sunday worship. This is not the case at St. Clement's, where the church was gutted in 1962 under the rectorship of the Rev. Sidney Lanier, a cousin of Tennessee Williams, and a theatre built in its place. On Sunday morning a portable altar, pulpit, and celebrant's chair are placed on the set of whatever play is running, and the drama of liturgy replaces the drama of the theatre.

Many performers, playwrights and directors have gotten their start at St. Clement's, including Sam Shepard, Al Pacino, Dustin Hoffman, Sam Waterston, and David Mamet. The liturgical side of St. Clement's has attracted worshipers as diverse as Corin Redgrave, Joan Baez, Kevin Spacey, Judy Collins, and Margaret Mead. This combining of theatre and religion is natural for those involved. "There is no enduring drama that does not have a theological message," said the former rector, the Rev. Barbara Cawthorne Crafton.

Connecting to a congregation, a mentor, or a good teacher can lead people on the journey to self-knowledge by affirming their gifts, DeChamplain says, just as cruel comments can distort the sense of self. "To have self-knowledge, one has to come to terms with their self-image. People give up on freedom of choice because they think they're doomed to failure. We grow up with language which describes us, language other people said about us. It distorts who we are and we can get disconnected in our pursuit of our own inclinations and desires. We're an aggressive society when it comes to beating up someone who hurts us, but we're passive when it comes to taking responsibility for knowing ourselves. We have to be self-validating, but we also come into true being in connection with people who have accepted us."

And we keep at it. "Self-knowledge is not a destination; it's always in process. As we become more aware, we become more fulfilled. It's like the life of the faith journey. We move toward what we were made to be."

This means never imitating another. "We can learn from a great actor, but we can't be that actor. All careers have virtuoso performers. Know who you are and live to the fullest out of that. If you're doing what is true for you, then even when you don't get parts, you're still doing what you're supposed to be doing. That doesn't erode the soul. The more self-awareness and self-knowledge you have, the less likely you will be destroyed. You may be disappointed, but your spirit won't be broken."

Community

How very good and pleasant it is
when kindred live together in unity!
~PSALM 133:1

We are a family;
We are so much more, than just you and I.
~TOM EYEN, *Dreamgirls*

THE IMPORTANCE of community is one of the first lessons God teaches us. In the second creation story of Genesis, God not only made man but gave him the gift of companionship as well. "Then the Lord God said: 'It is not good that the man should be alone; I will make him a helper as his partner.' So out of the ground the Lord God formed every animal of the field and every bird of the air, and brought them to the man to see what he would call them; and whatever the man called every living creature, that was its name. The man gave names to all cattle, and to the birds of the air, and to every animal of the field; but for the man there was not found a helper as his partner. So the Lord God caused a deep sleep to fall upon the man, and he slept; then he took one of his ribs and closed up its place with flesh.

And the rib that the Lord God had taken from man he made into a woman, and brought her to the man."

That was the start of the first community. And community has since become not only the way people unite but also a major way in which we connect to God. Msgr. James Turro, in an essay in the September 2002 issue of the prayer book *Magnificat*, writes about the "overarching group consciousness" in the Hebrew scriptures, especially the Psalms. "That is to say the fundamental relationship is viewed as being not primarily between the individual and God but between Israel (the community) and God. The primacy of community is in fact presupposed throughout all of the Old Testament. It is an out-and-out corporate mentality, a consciousness of belonging to a family." He cites the way God instructs Moses to include the whole nation when he talks to Pharaoh, imploring: "Israel my son, my first-born . . . Let my son go that he may serve me."

The New Testament shares that view of corporate personality, Turro writes, quoting St. Paul's letter to the Romans: "For just as in a single human body there are many limbs and organs, all with different functions, so all of us united with Christ form one body, serving individually as limbs and organs to one another." Turro says Paul draws out the implications of this doctrine in a letter to the Corinthians: "If one organ suffers, they all suffer together. If one flourishes, they all rejoice together. Now you are Christ's body, and each of you a limb or organ of it."

So the word of God in scripture teaches us the need to form communities. Theatre, which brings together the gifts of singers, dancers, writers, choreographers, lighting designers, costumers and so many others, is a community of talents. As T. S. Eliot wrote for his chorus in his 1934 play *The Rock*, "What life have you if you have not life together? There is no life that is not in community."

Michael McElroy knows this well. When he was a child in Cleveland, church was the center of his life and he loved singing gospel music in the choir. The sense of community he felt there is something he has re-created at each step of his life since then. As a student at Shaker Heights High School, he saw a way to combine the worlds of his predominantly white school with his black Harvest Missionary Baptist Church. He formed a gospel choir of multiethnic, multiracial singers, called it Mixed Emotions, and took it on tour around Ohio for two years. "It was an opportunity to open up a new realm for people by combining two different worlds. People tended to gravitate to people like themselves, so I fought to encourage people to connect through the music."

He again used music to bring people together as a student at Carnegie Mellon University, where he was named director of its gospel choir. That allowed him a link to his past and gave him a break from long hours spent in the drama department, working on crews for shows, rehearsing, and performing. "We were putting in twelve- to fourteen-hour days. We ate together and hung out together. The gospel choir exposed me to a different group of people. It gave me a connection to the outside world I grew up in."

McElroy connected to that world again after moving to New York. In 1993, three years after he arrived, Nephi Wimmer, an actor he had become friends with while performing in *Miss Saigon*, died of AIDS. It was McElroy's first experience of losing someone to the disease and he was devastated. "In the eighties when the AIDS epidemic was at its height, I was in college and it was not part of my world. I saw my good friend waste away to nothing." It made McElroy think about two deaths from his past—losing his father when he was four and his grandfather six months later. "It triggered issues of death I hadn't dealt with."

He sought out the healing power of music. He had done two cabaret performances of his own at Don't Tell Mama on New York's Restaurant Row, but felt he needed the music of his childhood. "I wanted to do gospel. That sustained me, and my connection to God I find through that music." He asked ten other Broadway actors to rehearse and do a gospel concert with him. Once again it was a mul- tiracial, ethnic, and religious group. Calling themselves the Broadway

Gospel Choir, they did the concert for Broadway Cares/Equity Fights AIDS, a nonprofit AIDS fundraising and grant-making organization. "The response was overwhelming. We decided to make it a yearly event. It grew in importance to the community." The reason, he says, is that gospel music is universal.

"It was born within the Baptist Church and had been considered for black audiences, so it was a joy to me to watch people discover for the first time the feeling of the inclusive power of the music. It's the truest expression of God. You can't escape the power of this music whether you're Jewish or Muslim. It crosses all barriers."

So once again McElroy had created community, and healing, through the power of music and had given Broadway its first gospel choir. But the harmony of that community was threatened when, as the group's recognition grew, the people handling the administrative side tried to take on more of the creative side, McElroy says. He hired a lawyer, racked up thousands of dollars in legal bills, and broke away to ensure he would be controlling the choir he loved. Because the production company had already patented the name Broadway Gospel Choir, McElroy renamed the choir Broadway Inspirational Voices.

"It was a life lesson," he says. "Sometimes you have to step up and say 'This is mine.' I loved that music and what it did for people singing in the choir." He doesn't place all the blame on the production company, saying things weren't always handled properly on either side. The real break was over vision. "They never got what this music is about. It was my life. It's what I grew up with."

Despite the troubles, McElroy was determined to go on. He continued to grow the community, asking people he had seen in shows or with whom he was performing to join. The choir, now with nearly fifty members, is about 60 percent black, 35 percent white, and 5 percent Latino and Asian and includes Catholic, Baptist, Presbyterian, African-Methodist, Episcopalian, Jewish, and Buddhist members. McElroy says the music transcends their differences. "It was born out of a place of pain and hope."

Performing mostly for charities and usually without pay, the choir is booked throughout the year, singing four major concerts and appearing at about a dozen events annually. It is McElroy's priority now in his career and even though he doesn't get paid for it, he regularly sacrifices work if it interferes with the choir's Tuesday afternoon rehearsals. His agent knows not to even think of scheduling an audition for him at that time. "I believe God put me here for a reason and gave me the gifts I have for a reason. That sustains me."

His belief and devotion have paid off. Broadway Inspirational Voices is now a full-time choir with a national reputation. The choir performed at the Tony Awards ceremony in 2000, for President Clinton at OpSail 2000, and at the lighting of the Olympic torch in 2001. They recorded a CD with Bob Dylan entitled *In the Garden* and in 2002 released their own CD, *Grace*, for which McElroy cowrote, with Joseph Joubert, two songs. In "The Storm Is Passing Over" he shares his belief that God cares, so we shouldn't give up or give in during difficult times. "Through the faith we will win. . . . The race is not given to the swift, but to the one who endureth to the end." "In God's Love" is about entrusting one's life to God. "Dear Lord above, I come to you in prayer, and at your feet, my burdens we can share. . . . I receive amazing grace, in God's love. Try him for yourself, there's peace, in God's love." The eleven songs on *Grace* were sung by forty-three singers from more than a dozen Broadway shows, including *The Producers*, *The Full Monty*, *42nd Street*, *Beauty and the Beast*, *Cabaret*, *Thoroughly Modern Millie*, *Into the Woods,* and *Mamma Mia!*

McElroy is grateful for the recognition Broadway Inspirational Voices has achieved because it means his work for the choir is paying off in the way he wants it to. "I'm not trying to make a name for myself. I get seen. When they're looking for an African-American male, I get called in. This is extra, to feed me spiritually. It's a way to give a gift to the community." Which was just what he had in mind long before he knew his choir would take off as it has. "It was at a time when we were lost. No one could understand the experience of pain we were going through in our community. I knew this music is a healing balm."

That healing balm was needed again in the fall of 2001 after the attacks on the World Trade Center. McElroy found directing the choir especially challenging because many members, their security so shaken, found it hard to concentrate. But for one member especially, those days following the attacks were a nightmare. LaChanze, who was eight months' pregnant with her second daughter, lost her husband, Calvin Gooding. McElroy and other choir members tried to be a source of solace and the choir donated money for her children's education. "It was hard to concentrate on what's important, to feel embraced by the spirit of God," McElroy says. "The music was a chance to know the love of God."

McElroy experiences that love not just in the music but also in the transformation of his choir members. "My back's to the audience so my concentration is on them. I can see the presence of the Holy Spirit and God in each and every one and how they are affected. That couldn't be without the presence of God." He is especially thrilled to see the change come over the Roman Catholics, Methodists, Jews, and others who have not grown up with gospel music. "You can't fake it and there's nothing you can do to make it happen. It comes from a sense of being vulnerable, open to the Holy Spirit moving in you. We all have different vocabularies of how we worship. It's interesting to see them wrestling with how to handle it when an experience comes over them. Sometimes they jump up or let the tears flow. That's part of my history."

Now it's part of Broadway's history too.

History also figures into Liam Neeson's consideration of theatre and community.

"The early actors were shamans," he said one April evening in 2002 in his sitting room at Broadway's Virginia Theatre before an evening performance of *The Crucible*, in which he was playing John Proctor. "They danced around the fire and tried to interpret what was out there to the tribe. They made a pathway, a connection to the ether. They would try to explain why there was a drought and be the spokesmen. They communicated with the spirit world. That's an extension of what actors do."

He felt that's what the cast was doing in *The Crucible* revival, which opened six months after the terrorist attacks. "The horror of September 11 awakened people to the real world of people with incredible anger and hatred. We blinded our eyes to it for a long time, not just in this country but all over the Western world. The play deals with fundamentalism and everything spiraling out of control. It's touching a chord in people they are emotionally responding to. Maybe within that is the answer to what we're all going through."

It's a shared experience, he says, of the twenty-one-member cast and the audience, which becomes the twenty-second member. "Everybody's incredibly focused onstage, the actors with each other and with the audience. It releases energy that is real." The power of this shared experience is important now as our world becomes more corporate and technologically advanced, he says. "There's an erosion of faith. People don't know what to believe anymore. Actors can give a focus. They can help show another facet of life."

They do this by taking people out of their routines, Neeson says. "They're storytellers. Maybe the faith is in the repetition of these stories. They're relived from one generation to another." For him, the experience can be sacred. "You're seeing a piece of heightened reality condensed into two or three hours. You get to see some person's dilemma and ask 'What would I do?' or you recognize the situation they're in. You're comfortable with the other audience members seeing it with you. It's a community; you're not in isolation."

This communal experience made him realize how much he loved doing theatre when he was appearing in "freezing little barns" in Northern Ireland in the mid-1970s. The casts were performing works by Yeats and other serious dramas for as few as ten or twelve people. "It was a bad time. Bombs were going off, but the theatre never closed. It was important that we were doing it, and the audience was there. It was something to celebrate life rather than the destruction all around us."

Neeson and McElroy both found healing in community, healing even in the face of violence and death. For Amanda Blair Ellis, community was central to her life growing up in the American South and helps shape her career now as an actor and producer in New York.

"I grew up very much in and through a Christian community," she says. "The music, the service and the community I grew up with in church is very much what I experience in the theatre. Going to church is about figuring out what it means to be human and that is what I search for in the theatre."

Ellis's journey began near Oxford, Mississippi, where she attended Sunday school at the Episcopal church and sang in the choir of the Methodist church where her grandmother was an organist for thirty-five years. Her summers were spent at Camp Bratton-Green, an Episcopal camp named for two former bishops, and she served on the diocese's youth board in junior and senior high school. That early experience of community made a strong impression. "My best friends were all from there. Once a month I was either on retreat or planning one." She then moved on with some of those friends to the University of the South in Sewanee, Tennessee, an Episcopal school where she majored in theatre and minored in music.

Years later, living in New York and working in theatre, she felt called to re-create the strong sense of community she had experienced in Mississippi. With a friend she created her own production company, TWP/Skydancer Productions, with the stated idea that "theatrical performances are a team effort, and are most fulfilling for the team AND the audience when the team works and plays well together." They have produced original work by, for, and about women. "I feel the whole is bigger than the sum of its parts," she says. "When you have a group of people working well together and trusting each other, creativity just explodes."

Ellis kept the production company rolling, but always made sure everyone felt involved. "They needed to be invested, too, to get something out of it. When people find a place where they're appreciated they are able to open themselves in a way they can't without that professionalism and integrity." She contrasted her company's goals with what happens when the producer can't be trusted or the cast is negative or cruel. "Then you have to choose when to use your art and when to protect yourself. It takes a lot of energy. When you find a place of trust, the art comes faster."

Unfortunately, she lost that place of trust in her church community. She had worshiped for years in a theatre-district Episcopal church where she sang in the choir. But when she went through a series of crises—two surgeries for possible cancers, trouble in her marriage, and other difficulties—she found the rector to be cold and fellow parishioners distant. The experience was so painful she stopping going to any church. "I found that a lot of my theatre and other artist friends who were not Christian or who didn't claim to be religious were treating me more in a Christian way than my friends at church and my priest. It was really a difficult blow. I've always gone to church." She considers herself now "in the stage of finding something new." She maintains a sense of community with her theatre friends and feeds her soul through yoga, dance classes, meditation, and journal writing.

Rabbi Irving "Yitz" Greenberg is a warrior on behalf of community-building, at times to the point of incurring severe criticism from fellow leaders in the Orthodox movement. His belief in community goes hand in hand with his respect for all individuals. He points out that in Judaism the individual is seen as being of infinite value, equal to all others and unique unto herself or himself. That is why the Talmud states, "If you save one life it is like saving the whole world," he says. Simultaneously, this worth is brought forth and sustained through the community, which has "a depth and capacity to sustain human value which no individual has." It is corporately that Jews carry out their "covenantal community," the partnership between God and humanity to perfect the world.

No individual alone can achieve that, Greenberg says. Using the Hebrew word *tzedakah* to compare the Jewish responsibility to the world with a person's responsibility to family, he argues that just as a parent must do for a baby which cannot take care of itself, so must Jews take care of the poor and the downtrodden. "Charity is given not out of compassion; it's an obligation. It's a sense of powerful connection, as close as our flesh and blood. What makes that so is community."

Because community is so essential, Jewish tradition calls for a minimum of ten people to gather for prayer in the practice known as *minyan*, or a counted number to pray collectively. "When we pray in community the prayers must be answered. They have a weight and reach no individual prayer can have."

A *minyan* does not make a community, though. "If ten sit in a room they are not yet a community. What makes a community is when they decide to pray and appoint a prayer leader. This act declares their common goal, and only then do they become a community of prayer." Greenberg defines a community as "a group of people united by a common purpose or destiny to which they are dedicated. Community is created by a sense of shared purpose, value, and direction." He says one could practice Judaism without the community, but "it would be more like a piece than the whole." And while this community sense has its roots in biblical days, as expressed in the Psalms and throughout the Hebrew scriptures, "that end of the biblical period was not the end of Judaism," he says. The Rabbinic period deepened the Jewish communal foundations of human dignity; individuals as individuals—rooted in community—are even more highly valued by the developments in Jewish tradition and thought in modern times.

Greenberg has devoted his life to creating community among the various branches of Judaism. Besides writing extensively on the subject of pluralism, he was a founding president in 1974 of CLAL: the National Jewish Center for Learning and Leadership, an organization that pioneered the development of adult and leadership education in the Jewish community and was the leading organization in intra-Jewish dialogue and work of Jewish unity. Now, as president of Jewish Life Network in Manhattan, his mission is to create new institutions and initiatives to enrich the inner life—religious, cultural, and institutional—of American Jewry. His longtime dream is to start a retreat center that will bring all branches of Judaism together. Professor Steven T. Katz wrote of Greenberg's work in the book *Interpreters of Judaism in the Late Twentieth Century*, "No Jewish thinker has had a greater impact on the American Jewish community in the last two decades than Irving (Yitz) Greenberg."

Pluralism is necessary to achieve the overarching Jewish goal of perfecting the world, Greenberg says. Disagreements can be recognized, even appreciated, but they should not be allowed to become sectarian and polarizing, because then they become so destructive they cause one group to reject another. "As Judaism exists in our time, we share the same fate and destiny. Persecutors do not distinguish between Jews. There should be mutual support. Israel made itself available when Jews were in trouble around the world. There should be a sense of common fate that prevents this kind of fighting. Like in a family, we have to make room for the other person. "

The drop in anti-Semitism and increased acceptance of Jews in American society have caused people to lose sight of the need for pluralism, says Greenberg, who was born in Brooklyn and holds a Ph.D. in American history from Harvard. "We're so well off and accepted that we feel comfortable at home and can now take off our gloves and fight. Our sense of security releases us from fear of the outside world, and then people think 'I want it my way.' So greater strife and less patience with each other is a paradoxical effect of Jews becoming mainstream in America."

His strong stands on behalf of community have had a price. He was attacked as a heretic before the Orthodox Rabbinical Council of America, which in the 1980s came close to censuring him. He also was prevented from speaking at Yeshiva University, where he chaired the history department from 1964 to 1972.

Others, though, see a need for pluralism. "There are many Jews who recognize the common concerns, that the danger of one translates into the danger of all and the safety of one involves the safety of all," Greenberg says. "We're a small minority in a large sea of accepting non-Jews. Therefore, freedom has generated a very powerful centrical force on American Jewry. By contrast, when we're united, we have a more powerful magnet—an attractive community—to hold people. The alternative to unity is disaffiliation, a real loss of connection."

Greenberg's ideal of community also includes women, whose role has been secondary in the Orthodox movement. His wife, Blu Greenberg, is president of the Jewish Orthodox Feminist Alliance. "Women are fully human and must be treated accordingly," he says, adding that a community loses the capacity of the people it excludes. "In creating a perfect world you can't start by wiping out the world and building a new one. You build the perfect one from within. Historically women were seen as second class, but we've got to move on and recognize their full talents and abilities. Tradition shouldn't be a cover for keeping things the way they are. Each community consists of men and women. To me it's self-evident that women have to be part of it. The trick now is to move up their status. They have great contributions to make. It's important to the whole community."

In a third area of community-building, Greenberg has created dialogues with Christians, Muslims, and the Dalai Lama. "In the end, it's humanity," he says. "The Bible starts with Adam. Adam was not Jewish. The community has different values, but never lose sight that it's a community of human beings. The religion of others is part of their value. You can't love people in general. You have to affirm their specific religion."

But Jews must never forget their own history, which is why Greenberg commuted back and forth to Washington, D.C., to serve as chairman of the United States Holocaust Memorial Council from 2000 to 2002. Before that he served as the first staff director of the President's Commission on the Holocaust in 1978, and prior to that he worked to make Holocaust studies an acceptable academic discipline; when his proposal to teach a course in the history of the Holocaust was rejected by Yeshiva University, he suggested a course entitled Totalitarianism and Ideology in the 20th Century, which was approved, and in it he taught his Holocaust course.

"The Jewish religion starts with the memory of the Exodus," he says, explaining that that event should remind Jews to help the poor and alienated because they also were once strangers. "That tradition of remembering continues through the people. The twentieth century was the most fearsome period of Jewish suffering. You remember the suffering so you can try to correct it for everyone. Community is the vehicle for transmission of these values; there is a persuasive power in the community that is beyond the capacity of an isolated individual. Furthermore, if our dream is to perfect the world, we can't do it in one generation. If it is carried in the community, then the community has the ability to pass it on from generation to generation."

The Rt. Rev. Catherine S. Roskam, suffragan bishop of New York, knows the strength of community in the theatre world and in the world of religion because she has experienced both, having spent sixteen years as an actor before becoming an Episcopal priest.

"The play is not the script, just as the liturgy is not the altar book," she says. "They are the tools so it can happen—in the context of community. It can't happen any other way. You can't recite a part;

you recite poetry. You *enact* a part, as you do in liturgy. That's why drama and theatre used to be the same."

Roskam became a community builder in 1972 when she formed the Joseph Jefferson Theatre Company for experienced actors who found their commercial work unsatisfying. They performed revivals of American plays, and members included Armand Assante and Rhea Perlman. The company was based at Manhattan's Church of the Transfiguration, an Episcopal church more commonly known as The Little Church Around the Corner, a nickname it earned following the snubbing of an actor in 1870. Out of that rejection came a legendary experience of community-building.

In December 1870 when Joseph Jefferson, a prominent actor of the day, was looking for a church for the funeral of a friend and fellow actor, George Holland, a priest of a nearby church agreed to host the service until he found out the profession of the deceased, a profession associated with loose living. He suggested Jefferson try "the little church around the corner," which the priest considered to have lower standards. The funeral was held there December 22, 1870, and the church gained not only a nickname but a large congregation of actors who began worshiping at The Little Church Around the Corner; they also were buried from there with respect. When Shakespearean actor Edwin Booth died in 1893, his funeral was held at the church, with Jefferson as an usher. When Jefferson himself died in 1905, his funeral was held in Massachusetts, but his memorial service at The Little Church Around the Corner was attended by a large number of well-known actors of the era.

And his memory lived on. Roskam ran the company she founded in his name and appeared in many of its productions, closing it in 1980 shortly before entering New York's General Theological Seminary. "It was great practice for becoming a priest," she says. "Actors have to subordinate their own egos and wills to the good of the larger whole just the way people in ministry do."

It also was great practice for a future community-building effort. After she was consecrated the first woman bishop in New

York State in 1996, she found herself in a House of Bishops she describes as "quite rancorous and divided." Her solution was to bring the bishops together into a choir. "We would never be of one mind, but we could be of one heart by making music together." Suddenly bishops who voted on opposite sides of issues were singing in harmony together. They became so good that in the fall of 2001 they recorded a CD of multicultural liturgical music called *With One Accord*. It is available through Episcopal Relief and Development in New York City, which receives the proceeds. Fundraising wasn't the goal, though, Roskam says. "We did it as a message and gift to the church so people could hear their bishops sing with one accord."

Learning to sing in one accord with other bishops wasn't such a stretch from performing with other actors in a play, she says. "An actor's life is very spiritual. It involves a lot of self-sacrifice and making the goal of the play foremost, not just one's own performance as an actor. The actor has to serve larger purposes."

At first she thought she was giving up the theatre community to become a priest, but she soon recognized the similarities between the two professions. "It wasn't such a new direction. It grew out of the theatre experience. It's all grist for the mill. I felt very strongly that theatre work is a calling, not just a job. You get a part sometimes, but many times you don't. But the call is always there."

For her, the call was leading her to serve God in a different way. "It's not something you decide to do and go after it, which was new to me because I am goal-oriented. It was a call that grew in me against my will. It evolved over a two-year period of discerning and resisting." The discernment evolved because actors and priests understand things in an organic way, she says. "An actor's training involves a lot of introspection, which is required on a spiritual journey. You have to find everything within yourself for an entire cast of characters of human emotions. It's like what the Desert Fathers believed— we carry within us the seeds of all humanity."

Actors also have a lot in common with those in monastic life who take vows of poverty, chastity, and obedience, she says. Except for those who hit it big, making ends meet is hard for actors. They don't practice chastity, but actors often have a hard time sustaining relationships because of their demanding schedules, with late hours and the need to be totally focused. And they must practice obedience. "They have to do what their director says, what their agent says. There's a discipline, a rule of life. They take classes, they dance. It's not unlike what people in religious life do."

And people in religious life have many of the same pressures as actors. "There's a public quality to ordained life they don't tell you about in seminary. You are up in front of people all the time. There's a kind of scrutiny of one's life that you would not have as an individual. There's also the role of the priest within the liturgy that is interpretive the way an actor interprets a play. Then you're naked in the pulpit sharing your faith and still interpreting the word. It's not just projecting your voice. It's the ability to communicate. Communication is a unifying endeavor."

Although her immediate responsibilities now involve overseeing sixty-six congregations in Westchester, Putnam, and Rockland Counties, much of her work is diocese-wide. She sees similarities between producing plays and being a bishop. "They both involve bringing something to fruition." Producers and bishops are visionaries whose work is implemented by others. "A bishop is a unifying factor and a connecting agent among congregations within a diocese."

In the Episcopal tradition, connecting in community is central. "We're part of the Anglican communion. They don't call it a federation. It is a community of churches throughout the world. It is a global community." She jokes that many people accuse Episcopalians of making a sacrament out of the after-church coffee hour, but she says that time is important for community-building. "We don't get our spiritual fix and go home. We're part of the Body of Christ. It's corporate worship. We participate as the people of God."

Hospitality

Even the sparrow finds a home
and the swallow a nest for herself where she may lay her young;
at your altars, O Lord of hosts,
my King and my God.
~Psalm 84:2

We've got magic to do
Just for you.
We've got miracle plays to play.
We've got parts to perform,
Hearts to warm,
Kings and things to take by storm,
As we go along our way.
~Stephen Schwartz, *Pippin*

WELCOMING THE stranger has always been a major element of both religion and theatre. Whether it's receiving a spiritual home before the altar or having our hearts warmed before the stage, hospitality is an essential gift of congregations and performers. Scripture gives us an early example. Abraham, in the eighteenth chapter of Genesis, entertained three strangers who appeared to him one day by the oaks of the Mamre. "When he saw them, he ran from the tent entrance to meet them, and bowed down to the ground. . . . 'Let a little water be brought, and wash your feet, and rest yourselves under the tree. Let me bring a little bread, that you may refresh yourselves, and after that you may pass on—since you have come to your servant.'" Under his direction, his wife, Sarah, and a servant prepared for them a feast of cakes of choice flour, curds, milk and a tender calf. When they were finished, "Abraham went with them to set them on their way."

The Hebrew scriptures are full of other examples of hospitality, along with the reminder that we are required to offer such treatment to others. In the gospels, Jesus tells his followers about the final judgment and the reward for those who practice hospitality. "Then the king will say to those on his right hand, 'Come, you that are blessed by my Father, inherit the kingdom prepared for you from the foundation of the world; for I was hungry and you gave me food, I was thirsty and you gave me something to drink, I was a stranger and you welcomed me, I was naked and you gave me clothing, I was sick and you took care of me, I was in prison and you visited me.' Then the righteous will answer him, 'Lord, when was it that we saw you hungry and gave you food, or thirsty and gave you something to drink? And when was it we saw you a stranger and welcomed you, or naked and gave you clothing? And when was it that we saw you sick or in prison and visited you?' And the king will answer them, 'Truly I tell you, just as you did it to one of the least of these who are members of my family, you did it to me.'"

In the performing arts world, the essential element for hospitality is the presence of the audience. While it might at first seem only the performers are giving hospitality by entertaining their guests, stage actors rely on the audience to give back to them through their laughter or expressions of emotion. Irving Berlin knew this when he wrote about "the audience that lifts you when you're down" in his great celebratory song "There's No Business Like Show Business" from *Annie Get Your Gun*.

"The give-and-take relationship with the audience dictates what the show will be," Kristin Chenoweth says. "I love it that no audience is always the same." She says a joke or piece of dialogue can go over great with an audience one night and be missed completely by a different audience the next night. "That's what's so great about theatre. It's like a love affair between the audience and the actors or the piece. Like a love affair, it doesn't always work." As a performer she tries to be mindful of this and treat each night's audience as guests with their own interests. "They give you a gift," she says. "You can feel it."

Actors Lesley Birchall Collis and Larry Collis also believe in practicing hospitality toward the audience, but they've taken it to an even greater extreme. When they decided to get married in 1979, they wanted to combine showbiz and matrimony, which isn't that unusual when two theatre people get together. What was unusual was that they chose to do it onstage at the Theatre for the Performing Arts in Phoenix, where Larry was appearing as Johnny in *The Unsinkable Molly Brown*. In what may be the height of actors' hospitality, they invited the forty-two actors and crew members—and the audience— to stay after the show for the ceremony. The show's director, Michael Barnard, developed a bad case of stage fright, but still managed to give away the bride, who was director of the career acting program at the Plaza Three Academy and who was not in the cast.

This post-show production included two other characters not part of *Molly Brown*, namely a Presbyterian minister who agreed to the unconventional location and a best man, John Clegg, who was musical director at the nearby Phoenix Little Theatre (now Theatre Phoenix) who sped up the second act of his show, *Gypsy*, to get to the ceremony on time. "The show's people did my makeup and hair and hid me backstage so Larry wouldn't see me," Lesley says. "It was fun." Then it was down the aisle in a sleeveless blue chiffon dress to meet the groom. Larry remained in costume and the headboard from the brass bed—a prop with its own song, " My Own Brass Bed"—served as the altar. The audience loved it.

The "cast party to end all cast parties" followed, with a cake, courtesy of the director, bearing the inscription "Make It Unsinkable, Lesley and Larry."

"We've always tried to share our home and activities with other actors," says Lesley about the decision to invite a theatre full of people to their wedding. "I love to entertain."

Loving to entertain is one thing when one is expecting the guests, but the Collises practice hospitality even when they aren't. Their most memorable experience happened shortly after they moved to New York in 1988 for Larry to appear in *Mail* on Broadway. They had been subletting the apartment of the show's lyricist and book writer, Jerry Kolcher, at Seventy-second Street and Columbus Avenue, a great location. But the apartment was in the back, shut off from any light by surrounding buildings, and furnished with little more than a futon and two plates.

When *Mail* closed after a short run, the Collises decided to stay on in New York, but in a different apartment. They sublet one at Ninety-second Street and Broadway from Mark Dovey, a dancer who was going to Toronto for a year to do *The Phantom of the Opera*. This one offered light, space, stained glass windows, and antique furniture. They were thrilled.

Having made the decision to stay, Larry reached out to Edward Asner, whom he knew from serving on the national board of the Screen Actors Guild while Asner was president; Asner (then best known for playing Lou Grant on the *Mary Tyler Moore Show*) was appearing on Broadway in a revival of *Born Yesterday*. Asner was delighted to hear the Collises were in town and suggested they throw a housewarming party to christen their new digs. An entertainer through and through, Lesley whipped up a Sunday evening gathering—ham, a crock pot full of baked beans, bread, cheese, salad, "stick-to-the-ribs actors' food that doesn't cost a lot of money"—to which Asner was invited.

Wanting to respect Asner and not treat him like a celebrity guest, the Collises didn't let anyone know he was coming. Turns out this was a good thing because Asner didn't show.

The next night as Lesley and Larry were lounging around the apartment, dressed in sweats, the doorbell rang. Who could that be, they wondered, only to find their belated guest. "Happy House, Collises," he shouted, giving them hugs and a beautifully wrapped Dust Buster. They were taken aback, but Asner just looked around and asked: "Am I the first to arrive?"

When they told him the party had been the night before, he was mortified until the ever-hospitable Collises fixed him a drink and Lesley began putting out the leftovers. Not just for Asner as it turned out, because he announced that he had invited a couple of friends—best-selling novelist Judith Krantz and her husband—who would be there shortly. Lesley imagined Krantz as someone who would have several villas and travel around the world and wondered what she would think of the non-doorman building on upper Broadway, but that didn't stop her from offering her own brand of entertaining.

After the leftovers had been eaten, it was Asner's turn to provide hospitality by saying he wanted to take them all out for dessert. They headed out, the Collises still in their sweats, to catch a taxi. Asner, who had driven a cab in New York while trying to get acting jobs, sat up front with the driver, asking him about his shifts and about his family, "the most human, caring, down-to-earth, old shoe person," Lesley says. At the time, it seemed pretty remarkable to her—two actors transplanted to New York, with a Broadway show just canceled and in a tenuous position, living in a sublet, riding with a high-profile actor, a famous novelist, her husband, and the taxi driver. "I thought, 'Wow, who would have thought all this would happen?'"

Asner directed the driver to O'Neal's, a bar/restaurant where he was greeted like royalty by the manager. "It was a very interesting evening, to say the least," Lesley says.

Since those early days in New York, the Collises have continued to entertain and, drawing upon the experience of their wedding, have found a way to combine show business and worship. At St. Malachy's/ The Actors' Chapel, Larry sings in the choir and Lesley is a lector, or lay scripture reader, during the Mass. Although neither is Catholic—Larry grew up Methodist and Lesley in the Church of England—both feel at home at St. Malachy's, just as hundreds of theatre people have through the years. Founded in 1902, St. Malachy's was the parish church for the largely Irish immigrant neighborhood west of Eighth Avenue. (St. Malachy was a twelfth-century Irish bishop.) But two decades later it saw its ministry changing. The theatre district had moved from Fourteenth Street to Midtown and the church's pews began filling with theatre people and tourists in town to see their shows. Recognizing a need to adapt to this new congregation, the clergy rearranged services with an eye on theatre and nightclub schedules and, in 1920, added The Actors' Chapel below the main church, with Masses at midnight and in the wee hours of Sunday morning. George M. Cohan, Spencer Tracy, Danny Thomas, Bob Hope, and Perry Como were among the many who worshiped there; Don Ameche, Pat O'Brien, and Jimmy Durante served Masses; Douglas Fairbanks and Joan Crawford were married there; and thousands jammed the sidewalk and street outside in a final tribute to Rudolph Valentino.

In later years The Actors' Chapel was moved upstairs and combined with the main church, but actors continued to come. Lighting a candle there before opening night is one tradition theatre people have passed down through the years. And for many of these actors, memories of St. Malachy's remain long after their hoped-for fame has arrived. Before its rededication ceremony in 1993, the church received a letter from Gregory Peck telling how he had attended Mass there and prayed for his first job. Others used the occasion of the rededication to express their appreciation for the hospitality they found at St. Malachy's. Lynn Redgrave wrote: "Our work requires *us* to rededicate ourselves again and again through the years. A visit to St. Malachy's has often given me the strength to do just that." Chita Rivera had similar thoughts. "St. Malachy's has been a great part of my life and life support," she wrote. "I have spent many hours of comfort through the years in this beautiful church and it has been a source of therapy, celebration, and meditation." Florence Henderson also expressed her appreciation: "It's very hard for me to put into words what St. Malachy's has meant to me. It was 'my church' and my place to go and regain my strength, my confidence, and my soul. It was where I first took my children to Mass, where I would go often between matinee and evening performances and where I would meet my fellow actors. I could never imagine Broadway without St. Malachy's. They are inseparable! I am with you all in spirit and my spirit will always be a part of St. Malachy's!!"

Sometimes the "guests" can't make it to the theatre—or a theatre congregation—because of physical or mental illness or disability. These people are part of the mission of DZIECI, an international theatre ensemble founded by actor Matt Mitler. Guided by Stanislavsky's maxim, "We must love not ourselves in art, but art in ourselves," the ensemble balances its performances with works of service through creative and therapeutic interaction with a variety of disadvantaged populations. DZIECI members believe that by helping others, a profound healing effect is generated that not only serves the patient but strengthens the ensemble's work as well.

"In a hospital or onstage, we create a community," says Mitler, who originally was trained in psychotherapy. "We need each other. It's a shared experience. The audience is thankful and, if we've done our work the right way, we feel thankful."

Most of DZIECI's members have a spiritual practice, says Mitler, who was raised Jewish but says he now embraces all religions, and theatre is their shared spiritual form. Besides their theatrical performances, all members must participate in outreach to the mentally and physically disabled. "We're using theatre as an act of service in the real Christian sense of the word. It also has a humbling effect on how we perform." These hospital visits rely on the group's expertise in clowning, acrobatics, choral singing, and trust exercises to establish a bond with patients, ultimately empowering them to join in the creative process.

The actors' approach is to always appear less advantaged, coming in with tattered costumes and goofy teeth. "If they're fearful, we're more fearful," Mitler says. From there the actors work to build the trust of their patients, who frequently are children with psychiatric problems. "We act like we don't know what to do, and then we try to do something and we can't do it." Then DZIECI comes up with an idea for some acrobatics or something for which they seek the patients' help. Gradually they get the children to fall off a table into their arms, then the children fall into each other's arms and finally the staff people into the children's arms. That final role reversal of the staff person trusting the children empowers the children with the pride of having caught her or him. "That trust goes on after the performance," Mitler says. "We leave and something changes. They see the therapist or staff person differently, and the staff person sees the patient differently."

For older patients who are in bed, the physical contact involves healing techniques and song. This was the approach DZIECI used while spending a Sunday at the Cabrini Center for Nursing and Rehabilitation on the Lower East Side of Manhattan. After assembling in a third-floor parlor to change into their sixteenth-century peasant costumes, made by the group's costume designer, Karen Hatt, they sat together for breathing exercises and rehearsed a fifteenth-century hymn in old French about waiting for Jesus. They then headed down the hall singing the Latin chant "Pange Lingua" and almost immediately were met by a tiny Spanish-speaking woman who began teaching them a hymn of her own, using her finger to direct them. She applauded enthusiastically when they finished, telling them "very good" in English and smiling broadly. They introduced themselves in Spanish and had a brief conversation before moving on, again singing "Pange Lingua" as they stopped to serenade four women in wheelchairs. The women at first seemed unresponsive, but the members continued to sing, gathering closer and holding the women's hands. By the time they were ready to move on, one of the members, Rebecca Sokoll, had her head in a woman's lap and was holding both of her hands. Before she left, Sokoll hugged and kissed the woman, who still did not speak but whose expression had changed from vacant to serene.

The ensemble members then moved together into rooms, in one kneeling beside a woman who was sleeping. She woke at the singing and looked startled at the people in peasant costumes gathered around her. When she appeared as though she would cry, Mitler put his hand on her forehead. Then slowly she pulled her hands from under the covers and the members all reached to hold them. "Thank you for coming," she said in a weak voice, "thank you." She blew them kisses as they slowly backed out.

DZIECI's hospitality was noted in a letter by Cabrini's past therapeutic recreation director, who recalled seeing DZIECI members lift a disabled resident from her wheelchair and carry her as if she were floating on water. "I have been unable to erase that image from my mind; and I hope I never forget it," he wrote. "Other residents responded to this work in a way that more traditional supportive techniques were unable to foster."

DZIECI members are paid only about half the time for their hospital visits, and then only nominally. They put up their own money for publicity and space rentals. Their theatre performances are on a donation basis because "we believe no one should be excluded," says Mitler, who puts food on his own table by writing, directing, designing theatrical lighting, serving as a private acting coach, and doing comedy. Ensemble members also are willing to barter; they did laundry for one theatre company in exchange for rehearsal space. "We come with nothing," Mitler says. "We're like vow-of-poverty monks."

Besides the hospitality that takes place between actors and audience, many theatre people recognize the need to practice it in their backstage world. Actor Carol-Jean Lewis is one of them. "There's always someone younger and they're so scared," she says. "They have all these preconceived ideas from books and school. They just reek of panic. I do my best to make them feel at ease and at home." She starts this on the first day of a new production when the cast gathers around a conference table and people introduce themselves. She grins at the young actors, makes small talk and jokes, and brings them a snack because she knows how difficult the profession can be. Her mother had warned her that a performing arts career could take its toll on her. "My mother said I was too sensitive and people would take advantage of me, which they did; but I survived it."

What Lewis does for young actors epitomizes Rabbi Allen A. Secher's definition of hospitality—"welcoming the stranger." Jews have been told in scripture to practice hospitality since ancient times, he says. "Historically the phrase appears over and over, 'Remember you were strangers in the land of Egypt.' We have a history of being an outsider, so we're told to remember what it was like and not countenance that any longer. That's why the phrase occurs so often. Almost every major biblical command is inclusive, of your manservant and your maidservant and the stranger in your gates, and how you treat them."

Secher heads a Jewish Renewal community, Congregation Makom Shalom, in Chicago. He says services there "take what's been and shake it up and give it a new flavor; and if that flavor means adapting it to the here and now, do it so it will have more sense in the twenty-first century." Worship services borrow from all three branches of Judaism. "Renewal has been attractive to those who feel disenfranchised. In our case the stranger is always welcome."

Jewish biblical history shows what happens when strangers aren't welcome, Secher says. "In Egypt, their being strangers got them into trouble. They were enslaved because they were looked on as strangers." History also provides a powerful role model in Abraham, whose story of welcome appears early in the Bible for a reason, Secher says. "Boy, if it was good enough for Abraham, it better be good enough for you."

Abraham didn't just offer food, Secher emphasizes, but he made sure his guests had their feet washed, which, considering they were in the desert, was more than just a courtesy. "He was saying, 'Let me honor you by washing your feet, by wasting my most precious resource, water. I'm going to take gold from the desert and honor you with my jewels.'"

The payback, and Secher says there always is one, is that the strangers tell Abraham and Sarah they will have a child, which they had thought was impossible. He paraphrases poet Danny Siegel's reminder of the Talmud command to always assume the person next to you is the Messiah waiting for some human kindness.

Secher works to extend that human kindness through his Renewal community and by reaching out to people of other faiths. He is a counselor to the Jewish-Catholic Dialogue Group of Chicago, a 550-couple support and educational group for interfaith couples, and an officer of the Dovetail Institute for Interfaith Family Resources. He also is a board member of Aleph, the umbrella organization for Renewal Judaism.

In addition to his religious efforts, Secher has been involved for decades in show business, or maybe more precisely the media world. For thirty years he was host of the internationally syndicated radio show *East of Eden*. As a television producer he has won seven Emmys, including one for the PBS special *Choosing One's Way*, about resistance in Auschwitz, which was hosted by Ellen Burstyn. His most recent program is *Facing Alzheimer's*, which looks at the disease in the African-American community.

Reaching out in all of these ways is part of practicing hospitality because the biblical mandate still remains. In fact, the example of welcome is to be performed on a weekly basis, Secher says. "In the Abramatic tradition, any stranger is welcome at the sabbath meal. That's part of the practice of having two twisted breads. The second is for the stranger so there will always be enough. The Talmud says to fly a flag out at mealtime in case anyone in the neighborhood needs to eat. It also applies to lodging. You are to put the stranger up in the synagogue if you do not have lodging in your home. It's a major tradition."

The tradition also is emphasized in Jewish holidays, Secher says, such as at Passover with the seder meal's inclusion that all who are hungry are to come and eat. "That's repeated every single year. That's a definitive statement. There's no fooling around, baby." Hospitality is again practiced in the fall harvest feast of Sukkot, when Jews build temporary ceremonial huts call *sukkah*, reminiscent of those used in the desert long ago. "Any stranger is invited to share and take meals there."

Secher says "tons of Jews are not honoring the hospitality tradition." This doesn't make them bad Jews, but they would be more complete Jews if they did, he says. When asked if Judaism could be followed without practicing hospitality, he is firm. "The answer to that is a big fat no. If Abraham is to be our role model, then if you're inhospitable, you're sort of failing the role model. If Judaism says all who are hungry come and eat and you're not following that, you're not following the tradition."

From Abraham to the present, following the tradition boils down to one simple idea, Secher says. "Hospitality really means there's a place out there where you're safe."

The Rev. Erno Diaz, St. Malachy's pastor, says if churches want to follow the scriptures they teach and preach, they will be hospitable. "Hospitality was the hallmark of Jesus," he says. "He was always welcoming everybody, children, women, the poor, social outcasts. Hospitality is basic in every ministry of the church if ministry means an extension of Jesus' ministry." He says the gospels mention many times how Jesus dined with his friends and followers. "It was always in the context of meeting people. The evangelists picked it up right away. They wanted to stress it because it's important."

It was important in the Hebrew scriptures as well, he says, citing an example from the second Book of Samuel which had been part of that day's Mass readings. King David brought the ark of God to the city of David "with rejoicing; and when those who bore the ark of the Lord had gone six paces, he sacrificed an ox and a fatling. David danced before the Lord with all his might. . . . So David and all the house of Israel brought up the ark of the Lord with shouting, and with the sound of the trumpet. . . . When David had finished offering the burnt offerings and the offerings of well-being, he blessed the people in the name of the Lord of hosts, and distributed food among all the people, the whole multitude of Israel, both men and women, to each a cake of bread, a portion of meat, and cake of raisins."

Diaz points out how comfortable people in the Hebrew scriptures were with dancing, calling it "an expression of the soul." He sees dance movements in the celebration of the Mass in the way the priest opens his arms to say, "Let us pray," and in the stepping right and left at the

altar. For him, it is choreography. "The church should be really hospitable to the way people express their souls. There needs to be guide-
lines, but it should be open. In scripture they do these things."

Hospitality is important because worship is not just about self and
God. "When you're in church it's a community. There's somebody
beside you. You need to recognize them." It helps, he says, to refer to
liturgy as "a celebration of the Eucharist" rather than the Holy Mass,
which sometimes can imply dryness and rigidity. "That gives it a new
dimension of meaning. It has to be like that, a celebration." He also
prefers the term "minister of hospitality" to "usher" and instructs these
ministers to be especially hospitable to newcomers. "I want to continue
the tradition of St. Malachy's as a welcoming church."

Because his church also bears the title "The Actors' Chapel,"
Diaz thinks St. Malachy's should be especially open to people's creative ways of expressing their souls. He is considering converting the
church's west chapel into a small theatre. "Our church should lead
other churches in the archdiocese to be a theatre church. We don't
have to have exclusively Catholic plays as long as there's a message,
something people can relate to about the message of the Lord and
his work."

Diaz says he must be respectful of members of the congregation
who question the appropriateness of theatre in church. One way to
do this is to remove the Blessed Sacrament, the consecrated hosts
Roman Catholics believe to be the Body of Christ, from the altar. He
thinks the church needs to go back to its roots when plays were regularly performed in churches. "In the past, people were always comfortable with this," he says, explaining that the relationship between
theatre and religion is close. "Church liturgy is public performance.
It's theatre. The main actor is Jesus Christ. The lay ministers all have
a role to play. It's performance. The altar is like a stage in a little theatre, so let's incorporate theatre into the church. That's my desire for
St. Malachy's."

Ritual

The Lord is God,
and he has given us light.
Bind the festal procession with branches,
up to the horns of the altar.
~PSALM 118:27

Whenever I feel afraid
I hold my head erect
And whistle a happy tune
So no one will suspect I'm afraid.
~OSCAR HAMMERSTEIN II, *The King and I*

CREATING RITUALS is what we do for the significant events in our lives. We have our ways of celebrating holidays and commemorating tragedies, with the familiarity of rituals bringing us joy and comfort. Rituals also are part of our religious worship; we light candles, burn incense, blow horns, and carry through in an established order. Theatre proceeds in a similar way, with the rituals beginning even before the audience arrives. As Maria says in *Master Class*, Terrence McNally's 1995 Tony Award–winning play about opera star Maria Callas: "Attention must be paid to every detail. The light. Your wig. The amount of stage dust. A career in the theatre demands total concentration. One hundred percent detail." Then the performance itself is ritualized: "There are no shortcuts in art, no easy ways," she says. "This isn't life, where there are so many. There is no being at center stage as if by magic. There is always the entrance first, just as there is always an exit after." In between, the magic—and the transcendence—can happen, but it is shaped by traditional rituals to bring it into being.

Rituals also help us work by giving focus to a task; going through the motions readies us for the endeavor. For actors, performing certain rituals before going onstage helps them get over stage fright and also gets them back into a role, which can be especially helpful before the evening performance on two-show days. Most have a light meal and a nap between shows; many then develop ways to click back into character, like putting on makeup and wig in a certain order, saying a prayer, or sitting in silence.

Carol-Jean Lewis's rituals begin before she leaves her apartment in New York's theatre district. She bathes, spends time in silence with God, listens to gospel music, and reads her Bible. "I'm at peace and centered so when I leave here I'm better equipped for the darts Satan throws." This enables her to deal with people who may jostle her on the street or make negative comments at the theatre. "I can still see the God in them. I get prayed up before I go out so I don't get affected."

She arrives a half-hour to forty-five minutes prior to the half-hour before curtain when actors are required to sign in and does exercises to loosen her body. Then in that last half-hour before show time, she puts on her makeup and becomes whatever character she is playing. In the final five minutes before she walks onstage, "I go to

Jesus to cleanse me and offer up the gifts he has given me to bless whoever sees me and my fellow actors."

Staying grounded in God is the only way she can make sense of spending a life in show business, a life that for her has included the Broadway productions of *Daddy Goodness*, *Savara*, *Two Gentlemen of Verona*, and *Purlie* as well as numerous Off-Broadway productions. Her films include *Beloved*, *Quiz Show*, *Spike of Bensonhurst*, and all the voices for *Hairpiece: A Film for Nappyheaded People*. On TV she costarred in *The Days and Nights of Molly Dodd* and has appeared on *One Life to Live*, *Third Watch*, and other shows.

"What I do would seem frivolous and of no consequence if I didn't have faith the gifts God has given me have value to enlighten and heal if I stay out of the way and let God take over." That groundedness is also the only way she can get through the time between jobs when actors have to look for work, always holding themselves out for approval and facing a great deal of rejection. "Very few people get over the audition process. It's nerve rattling, but it hit me that God is my source so I'm not concerned whether I'm accepted or not."

Rituals help her to attain this peace, as a performer and as a person. Her attraction to ritual as a religious practice goes back to when she was twelve. Until then she had been raised as a Methodist in a family where religion was important; Lewis and her two older siblings couldn't go out to play if they didn't go to church. "My mother believed that a mother carries the child's sins until the child is twelve, then you have to go out and find your own way." Lewis found her way to Roman Catholicism. "When I went to the Catholic Church, it was so beautiful with the rituals and incense." She became a Catholic for six years. "I thought I wanted to be a nun until I experienced racism. That hurt me so bad. It was in the sixties and I found only one convent where blacks were accepted. I dropped out altogether."

Now she considers herself nondenominational and her worship ritual includes rising at 4 A.M., without an alarm clock, and watching televised ministries until 9 A.M. each weekday and until 11 A.M.

on Sunday. On Saturdays she rewatches the shows she has recorded during the week. "I've learned more through televised ministries than I ever would have in church. I support them. It's really a personal voyage with our faith. It's why I have cable. Now I have church seven days a week."

She turns off the preachers who don't ring true, and she gets her experience of community, usually a big part of regular churchgoing, from praying with her friends, all of whom watch television ministries.

A final element of her home worship is something she's done for more than three decades—keeping three candles burning. The white one in the living room is to purify her life, the green one in her bedroom is for prosperity and healing, and the yellow one in her daughter's room is for joy and understanding. They burn for seven days and at the end of that time she lights new ones, reciting by heart Psalm 91 for the white, Psalm 61 for the green, and Psalm 112 for the yellow. "I pray for everyone I love and people who don't love me. I spend three-quarters of the day with God when I'm not working. Working is almost inconvenient. I really enjoy this time when I'm free."

Merwin Goldsmith, a Conservative Jew, also grew up in a religious family and thinks anyone accustomed to religious rituals and their symbolism is especially open to an acting career, particularly someone who has participated in those rituals as an altar server or student cantor. "A preponderance of actors have had religious backgrounds," he says. "Anybody with a religious upbringing can make an easy transfer from religious practice to theatrical practice. You have an understanding of ritual."

Goldsmith—whose lengthy credits include radio dramas, television, films, Broadway, Off-Broadway, regional, and English theatres—remembers the rituals of his childhood in Detroit. His mother cleaned and cooked in preparation for the sabbath. Friday night meant lighting candles and Saturday morning meant going to the synagogue with his father, dressed in his best clothes, which included knickers, he laughingly confesses. "Everything went at half pace the rest of the day. It was a time for contemplation, things we didn't do during the week. I never did schoolwork then. That atmosphere and mood, if you've lived them in your own life, it's easy to transfer onto the stage."

As a member now of Park Avenue Synagogue, Goldsmith still worships weekly except when he's working. And although he doesn't keep kosher, he won't eat "the things Jews martyred themselves for," such as pork, or "things that crawl in the sea," like shrimp or crabs.

He has his rituals when performing, too. Although he has observed that many actors either "pray or puke" before going on, he does neither. "I think of the task in front of me. It's a way of calming myself. I think of the first, second, and maybe third thing I have to do, like walk onto the stage, cross to the table and pick something up. That gets me focused. There's spiritual experience in the mundane. That's the way I do my life as an actor."

Goldsmith has his rituals even before he gets onstage, which include reading a script over and over. "After a while it starts talking to you and tells you things about the character." As for being able to memorize so much dialogue, his ritual is to attach feelings to the words. "We deal in emotions. That's really what we're doing. By doing the work I do I make discoveries about myself and the people in my life. Working on a character brings an awareness of something in my life I wasn't aware of."

In this way ritual can lead to transformation. "If I say a line a number of times in rehearsal, I understand it in a way I haven't before. That's also part of the mystery of the talent. There's a lull, a quiet, then all of a sudden an actor does something monumental and it comes alive. There are moments like that in rehearsal. You don't push for it, you allow it to happen."

Going through the ritual of reading and rereading and speaking the part again and again, the ritual of the mundane, is what allows the breakthrough moments to happen, Goldsmith says. "Acting is a talent. What that talent is is not a mystery. Where it comes from is. It's scary sometimes because you seem to be in touch with something beyond you. You're hit with emotions or feelings that have been buried so long and maybe you can't identify the source of them. It's that touch of the divine. It's a little scary to get close to something really powerful."

For actors in DZIECI, an international experimental theatre ensemble based in New York, ritual is essential to their work as a company and as individuals, says founder Matt Mitler. "One very defined ritual in our work, whether it's in a hospital or theatre, is that before we begin we gather together in a circle and we're silent and still for a period of time as a way of searching inwardly and paying attention to where we are as a group. We want to leave the past behind and the future alone and come in fairly much with a clean slate." At the end of the performance, DZIECI members again gather in a circle of silence. "We want to feel the vibrations of what we've just done and measure our state of energy from what it was before to what it is now, to see if it's moved in an evolutionary manner, if it's finer or coarser, and to check our movement on the path."

Mitler says this ritual is part of his own self-study. "I feel the energy in my chest and heart, an openness. That's my litmus test. We do it for self-change. If I have a transformational experience of some sort, then the audience has a similar experience. If I'm false, it's manipulative. It always comes down to us working on ourselves."

This working on themselves is twofold. Nearly all of the fifteen members have their own spiritual paths, which include Buddhist and Native American practices. Mitler encourages this as a way to look inward and grow in self-awareness. The second part of working on themselves involves group activities in which ritual plays a large role.

Four times a year, at the change of each season, DZIECI members spend time in upstate New York at a Native American sweat lodge. In a day-long process, they gather stones, chop wood for their fire, and prepare the hut-shaped lodge for the ceremony. With earth-based prayers to honor the six directions—north, south, east, west, above, and below—and sacred hymns from the eighth to the sixteenth centuries, which they use in theatrical performances, the ceremony includes silent blessings for each of the stones they add to the fire. Each part of this three- to four-hour purification ritual, including the chopping of the wood, is performed "with prayer and attention," Mitler says. "The singing in the lodge at the peak of suffering of the heat is transformational. It's a way of bonding. *Anything* shared is a way of bonding. We could go bowling and it would be bonding, but this is deeper."

As a group they also have attended Sufi, Christian, Jewish, and Hindu ceremonies, but they like to create their own rituals as a path to empowerment. Mitler says the human potential movement of the 1960s and 1970s influenced him in this direction. "It's a way of facing fears and finding blocks in order to move past them to find other blocks. We like to ritualize as much as we can. We're interested in rituals that are alive."

They've also experimented with different rituals in eating together, which have included dining in silence, feeding each other, and moving in slow motion. "We experiment in the community to see what we can learn about ourselves under new conditions." Other rituals have involved the senses, being blindfolded all day and spending a day in silence. "We want to see ourselves in extreme conditions. How far out can I go and what do I need to come back? We're creating rocky waters."

Out of some of these experiences, workshops for the public emerge. Mitler calls the workshops "active meditation for four hours" and likes to offer them shortly after a theatrical performance so theatergoers have a chance to join DZIECI if they are interested. No one is asked to audition. "Your resume has little value to me," Mitler says. "We trust that the right people will stay and add to the equation, but it is not easy."

Another DZIECI ritual is writing in a shared journal. Each week a different member has the journal to express comments about performances or rehearsals and how he or she has been affected. Like Mitler, some DZIECI members had left show business for a time because they found it too ego-driven.

To keep their egos in check, the performers never take a curtain call. "Applause breaks the spell the ritual casts," Mitler says, quoting an African proverb. "We all wish to do work of a spiritual nature. For various reasons we find theatre is the best vehicle for us. We left because it wasn't fulfilling, yet we were pulled to do something about it."

For Mitler, using ritual as a way of developing his art is the culmination of a religious journey that began when he was growing up in Newport, Rhode Island. He attended Hebrew classes three nights a week and studied the Bible on Sundays at Touro Synagogue, the oldest synagogue in America. Although it is Orthodox, his family was not. They observed the holidays, but Mitler "never had a strong feeling about Judaism as a spiritual practice." He did, however, have a strong feeling for the rabbi, Theodore Lewis, who was from Ireland and whose spiritual nature appealed to Mitler. "He had a strength of purpose, a generosity of spirit, and a vibrant presence. I've sought out people of that nature my whole life."

His searching led him to humanistic psychology, experimental theatre, and Native American rituals. Then in Europe in the late 1970s, he learned about G. I. Gurdjieff's practice of integrating mind, heart, and body to create a "fourth way." He has been working on this now for nearly two decades, whether attending a formal religious service or in his own private practice. "I wish to use what I have to serve something higher."

In Judaism, serving something higher happens through ritual, says Rabbi Noach Valley, formerly the spiritual leader of Congregation Ezrath Israel/The Actors' Temple in New York's theatre district. "The purpose of ritual is to get closer to God and closer to people. Ritual is supposed to reflect inner meaning. Every ritual is to remind us to be more ethical and honest, moral and compassionate."

Ritual is related to the divine commandment known as the *mitzvah*. The Torah lists 613 commandments, 10 of which are the well-known Ten Commandments. They fall into two categories, what one does for other people and what one does for God.

Judaism could not exist apart from ritual, Valley says. "When you do ritual, you need to feel it's a command from God. You're doing God's will. It's a connection to God, not a burden, but a privilege."

Among the rituals of Judaism is the practice of praying three times a day. These routine prayers are in the category of *keva*, and should be done with *kavvanah*, a concentrated effort to put one's self into the moment. "*Kavvanah* should go together with *keva*, putting yourself into the routine." Informal prayers throughout the day also are encouraged.

Another form of prayer in Judaism is the *berakhah*, a word often translated as blessing, which Valley says is inadequate. He refers to *berakhah*, which ideally should be said at least one hundred times a day, as "a mystical formula of showing gratitude to God." It is often associated with eating, saying the formula before a meal and saying an entire series of them afterward. "If you eat food without thanking God you're stealing from God." These prayers of gratitude also should arise when we see something beautiful, "a rainbow, a mountain, the seashore, a scholar," Valley says. "It's like a wow, but moved over to divine experience. God is the source of everything we have. It's that human experience translated to the divine."

The rituals associated with Jewish prayer include the strapping on of *tefillin* for morning prayer. A sort of black box, it is put on the forehead "to show we belong to God in the sense of getting married to Him."Valley compares it to the way many Roman Catholic nuns wear wedding rings symbolizing they are married to Christ. "It's like being 'branded' to God in a loving, symbolic sense, to ritually demonstrate that we belong to Him, not as slaves, but as servants." Every traditional male over thirteen, and in some circles females as well, does this to symbolize giving one's mind to God. In a similar way strapping *tefillin* on the left arm next to the heart symbolizes giving the heart to God. In addition to representing the giving of mind and heart to God, wearing *tefillin* reminds the observant Jew to "judge one's self, to scrutinize one's deeds, and to deal with people in a more loving and ethical way,"Valley says.

Another ritual of morning prayer involves wearing a prayer shawl known as a *tallit*. Its fringes are tied in four corners in a special way to represent the 613 divine commandments. "The ritual is to remind you of all the commandments you have to do as a Jew." Valley compares it to the practice of tying a string around your finger. "Ritual comes from faith. One has the faith and trust and they are strengthened through ritual. You're part of a totality. There's a sense of belonging."

The converse also is true. Valley says if a person doesn't have faith but performs the rituals as if he does, faith can develop from that experience. Contrary to the popular idea that we act according to the way we feel, Valley says Jewish teachings and modern scientific research show actions producing feelings. "If at first you do attend synagogue, study Torah, light Shabbat candles, or make *kiddush* (the prayer formula to inaugurate the Shabbat or festival), there is a good chance the mood will follow, the emotions will surge, the deep feelings will take hold of you, and you will have the desire to continue to do these things,"Valley said in a 1999 Rosh Hashanah sermon, later published in booklet form and distributed to congregation members, service attendees, and colleagues.

In that sermon Valley said Jews should not wait until they feel like it to say the *berakhah*. "Instead, the *berakhah* is intended to produce feelings of awe, reverence, and spirituality and to help us experience the sublime joys and natural wonders that God's universe has to offer us in abundance."

Going through the rituals also helps one follow the command of the Torah, in Deuteronomy 6:5, to love God. Valley quotes Rabbi R. Kimelman, who says what actually is commanded "is immersion in the love relationship in the hope that love cannot long be enacted without being felt. Intensely going through the motion can produce the corresponding emotion, for actions beget reactions." This process has deep roots for Jews, Valley preached. "When we receive the Torah at Mount Sinai, we respond by saying *naaseh v'nishma*, meaning first we will act, and *then* we will analyze."

Valley says the Torah also commands people on eleven different occasions to be happy and rejoice before God. "It seems odd that the Torah can realistically command every Jew to be joyous. Is it possible to produce such an emotion on demand? The answer is yes, when we consider the fact that the command went hand in hand with eating and drinking, conjugal relations, praising God and bringing sacrificial offerings, and anointing oneself with oil and wearing vestal garments. The action, in this situation the doing of the *mitzvah,* made it easy to feel the reaction, here being the joy that was commanded by God."

He related the view of Judy Deylin, an actor member of the congregation, who says this method is similar to that taught in the early 1900s by Russian theatre director Konstantin Stanislavsky who told his students not to wait until they felt inspired but to act first and be inspired later. "More concretely," Valley preached, "action is within human control; inspiration or feeling is not."

As a Broadway example, Valley quotes Anna when she arrives in Siam in Rodgers and Hammerstein's *The King and I*. Anna's ritual when she is afraid is to hold her head erect and whistle a happy tune.

"The result of this deception, is very strange to tell, for when I fool the people I fear, I fool myself as well."

In his more than eight years as spiritual leader of The Actors' Temple, Valley followed traditional rituals and created some of his own. One of these involved carrying an empty chair from the altar out to the sidewalk on Forty-seventh Street during the Friday evening service. Worshipers inside joined in song as the chair was brought back, symbolically occupied by the Sabbath Queen. Valley called his Friday night service "traditional liturgy set to interactive theatre." Its debut in March 1997 attracted two hundred worshipers to the Conservative synagogue, the largest turnout Valley had had for a Friday service in his three decades as a rabbi.

The practice of welcoming the Sabbath Queen in this way is part of the Jewish mystical tradition known as *kabbalah* and derives from Safed (*S'fat*) in northern Israel. Other elements of *kabbalah* in the Friday service were guided visualization, singing, and dancing.

While the Sabbath morning service remained traditional, Valley took a slightly different approach there as well, by having "interactive learning" after the reading of the Torah portion (*sidra*) and using traditional commentaries to help his congregation understand their lives as modern Jews.

Valley thought of the music in his "nontraditional" Friday service in terms of letters, not R & B, but R & J—"rhythm and Jews." The ninety-minute service included a healing time in which worshipers could place their hands on one another or picture someone they knew who was in need of healing. They prayed together the shortest prayer in the Torah—"God please heal him [or her]." Valley then led them through guided visualization. He asked the congregation members to close their eyes, loosen tight clothing, uncross their legs, breathe deeply and slowly, and "shut out all extraneous thoughts and distractions."

With this readiness, it was time for the *sidra*, dealing with offerings brought to the altar for the purification of the worshipers. Valley instructed his worshipers to visualize themselves approaching the ancient altar, standing before God with deep humility and contrition, "love of the Almighty drowning out love of selves."

Next they were asked to see themselves as archers, carefully aiming at a target, pulling back their bow, but missing their mark. "This missing the mark is a metaphor for our human mistakes, not living up to our capabilities," Valley said quietly. He asked them to make a mental list of the ways they have missed their marks in things they have done and left undone, and how and when they could make amends. They sat still and again were asked to visualize pulling back the arrow in its sling. "This time visualize yourself scoring a direct hit, a bull's-eye right on the mark."

A third visualization involved picturing all their negative emotion as rising up in a smoky cloud and out through their noses. "Visualize any problems, depression, or stress being reduced to ashes," Valley said, adding that they should feel purified and closer to God.

The *Shema* prayer, which Valley calls the Jewish love song to God ("Listen, O Israel: Adonai is our God, Adonai alone"), was uttered while breathing in and out with each syllable. Valley gave a final exhortation as he left the sanctuary: "I want to remind you to keep smiling. When you're smiling, the whole world is Jewish."

Congregation Ezrath Israel was founded in 1917 as the West Side Hebrew Relief Association. Its leaders were Orthodox Jews who owned shops in the neighborhood. They borrowed a biblical name for God, *Ezrath Israel*, "the One who assists Israel," in naming their Jewish community center. "As the acting community came to New York, they migrated to the synagogue," Valley says. "All famous and not-so-famous Jewish actors came here." And so the name The Actors' Temple was added.

In its glory days, The Actors' Temple was one of the predominant synagogues in New York. Stars gathered every year for a gala fundraiser at one of the Shubert theatres. Among those who considered The Actors' Temple their spiritual home were Edward G. Robinson, Eddie Cantor, Joe E. Lewis, Sophie Tucker, Shelley Winters, Jack Benny, and

Jules Styne. Valley says they weren't all religious, but they showed up for High Holy Days, other holidays, and special occasions.

Over the years as more and more actors moved to Hollywood, attendance dropped. The mom-and-pop store owners in the neighborhood who had made the Temple the focal point of their lives died and their children moved out of the area. But The Actors' Temple's showbiz past will never be forgotten. Many of the stars are still present as names on stained glass windows and plaques on the sanctuary walls, and now, as then, the rituals continue.

Rituals continue in the Christian faith as well. The Rev. Canon Jay Wegman, formerly the Canon for Liturgy and the Arts at the Cathedral Church of St. John the Divine in Manhattan, says rituals are integral to liturgy and theatre because they are tied into myth. "Rituals can't be separated from story, whether it's a plot enacted in a play or a broader story through the liturgy."

Wegman's role at the Episcopal cathedral, the world's largest gothic cathedral, was that of master of ceremony for the liturgies, working with all the various participants, such as acolytes and altar guild, and overseer of the Cathedral's extensive visual and performing arts programs. He says rituals provide a framework, what he describes as a room in which to work. This room has doors that look into other rooms. "The room in which we live informs our story and ties into the larger world," he says. "When individuals come together through ritual, they are still individuals, but they are part of a collective self."

He cites the sacraments as examples. An individual baptized in water is still an individual, but through the ritual becomes a member of the church. In the Eucharist, "we come as individuals and share bread and wine and a much bigger feast. That celebration transcends time and space. There's a mystical element wrapped up in our rituals as well. Rituals move the everyday world to a larger realm.

Rituals are tools, defined pathways that help us become who we are meant to be."

All our major life transformations have rituals, he says. Birth is marked by baptism; confirmation is a rite of passage in which the individual reconfirms her or his faith to the larger body of believers; weddings take the individual story to the collective; and death has the rituals of last rites and funerals. "We use them as important turning points in our lives to move from one point to another."

The Cathedral has been host to many large-scale rituals. Wegman has planned services involving presidents Bill Clinton and Nelson Mandela, actors Vanessa Redgrave and Patti LuPone, and many other boldface names. "It's certainly the biggest sacred theatre in New York City, and certainly the biggest Off-Broadway house." But sometimes even that isn't big enough. In 1997 Wegman arranged the Cathedral's memorial for Princess Diana, which was held in Central Park for an estimated 25,000 mourners and featured the New York Philharmonic and opera star Jessye Norman.

These opportunities feed his priestly vocation and his love of theatre, both of which blossomed while he was growing up in Minnesota. When he was in third grade his mother took him to a high school production of *The Sound of Music*, which he thought was "kind of like church, but more fun and prettier." That was also the year he wrote to the Episcopal diocese of New York telling them he wanted to be a priest. "I was fascinated by church and things religious and by musicals."

In the summer of 2002 Wegman found another way to combine those interests. With the Very Rev. Harry H. Pritchett, a former dean of the Cathedral, he developed and taught "Putting It Together: Theology and Contemporary Musical Theater," a three-and-a-half-day course at New York's General Theological Seminary. Students saw *Oklahoma, Urinetown: The Musical* and *Into the Woods*, which were chosen to give them a variety of experiences, *Oklahoma* being a traditional musical, *Urinetown* a spoof of everything from traditional musicals to corporate greed, and *Into the Woods* falling somewhere in between.

Pritchett started the sessions the first morning by telling students not to worry about looking for complex messages in the shows. "Don't worry about the reading-in stuff," he said. "We're not doing systematic theology. I think theology is the transcendent or God-meaning we give to experience. That's what we'll be experiencing in these shows."

That God-meaning found in theatre is what rituals help us find in worship. But Wegman, who holds a master's degree in religion and the arts from Yale University, says it is important to see rituals as tools in the faith journey and not lose sight of the larger story. "I think rituals deepen the experience of faith. I wouldn't say you can't have faith without them. If you have ritual alone, you set up a false god."

What makes rituals helpful, he says, is that they can be used so creatively. He cites the Eucharist, which in his Anglican tradition follows the form set out in *The Book of Common Prayer* but which can be molded for different uses. On the first Sunday in October, the Cathedral is host to thousands of people and their pets for its annual Blessing of the Animals, commemorating the feast day of St. Francis of Assisi. St. Francis Day features the "Missa Guia," or Earth Mass, performed by the Paul Winter Consort; liturgical dancers; and a procession of animals, which in years past has included an elephant. It's a major New York event, "but the structure is the same as the simple Eucharist we have at 8:30 every morning. Ritual is an outline that can be embellished with all kinds of wonderful things. Creativity is essential to ritual or else it becomes dreary and leaden and serves little purpose. Ritual and liturgy are living, growing processes rooted in tradition, but they need to be connected to contemporary issues or else they're just detached things we do."

Transformation

Create in me a clean heart, O God,
and put a new and right spirit within me.
~PSALM 51:10

Hey, can't you just feel the strange excitement?
The quiet commotion that we share.
There's something like tingling in the darkness.
There's something electric in the air.
~STEPHEN SCHWARTZ, *The Magic Show*

THE STRANGE excitement and feeling of something electric in the air are among the qualities that make live theatre a transforming experience. Aristotle likened it to worship, calling theatre an "essentially religious ritual" with the audience in the role of communicants. He addressed the idea of transformation in his definition of tragedy: "Tragedy is an imitation of an action, that is at once serious, complete, and of certain magnitude, embellished with every kind of literary device, these devices appearing in various parts of the play, told in action, not narration, through pity and fear causing a catharsis of emotions."

Centuries later, Polish director Jerzy Grotowski summed up the transforming power in this way: "Art is a ripening, an evolution, an uplifting which allows us to emerge from darkness into a blaze of light." And Noel Dermot O'Donoghue, in *Heaven in Ordinarie*, expressed the healing possibility when he wrote: "What great art gives us most of all is companionship in our loneliness."

Religious services—like theatre—also help us emerge from the darkness and give us companionship in our loneliness. Msgr. Michael C. Crimmins came to understand theatre and its connection to liturgy in the decade he spent as pastor of St. Malachy's/The Actors' Chapel. "People in the theatre recognize the possibility of a moment of transformation," he said. "There's an appreciation of the Christian doctrine of grace, of glimpses of something more than we see on the surface of things. There are moments in the theatre when people are touched and changed, and that is like the experience of worship."

The audience is changed, but so quite often is the performer. "Far more important than the poem is what the poet becomes in writing it," Ralph Waldo Emerson said, expressing a sentiment that also could apply to actors. Similarly, French philosopher Michel Foucault asked: "Why should a painter work if he is not transformed by his own painting?"

Kristin Chenoweth knows that transforming power, and she has experienced it in both worship and theatre. Her encounters began long before her appearances on Broadway, in concert, and on television. They began as a child at the First Baptist Church of Broken Arrow, Oklahoma, where, because her voice was so advanced for her age, she performed alone. "I was singing in church before I knew what I was singing."

Her audience grew beyond that initial church group as she was invited to sing in churches across Oklahoma, and when she was twelve she sang before ten thousand Baptists at a convention. That's when she really felt the transformation of a gifted performance. "I remember feeling complete," she says. "I don't remember a big, huge thing. That's what it is, that's worship."

Chenoweth has had many more transforming experiences as a performer since then, having gone on to become a Tony Award–winning actress in 1999 and star of her own television series in 2001. She has tried hard to make sure her audiences are transformed, too, which is why she called her first solo CD *Let Yourself Go*. It has three original songs but also classics by the Gershwins and Rodgers and Hart, recalling a time many people now consider to have been simpler. "I wanted it to sound good, of course, but I really wanted it to be about the words, like I'm in your living room singing to you, not at you. I want people to be able to remove themselves, to enjoy it and have fun."

John Lahr, *The New Yorker*'s senior drama critic, describes the CD as Chenoweth's "Platonic ideal of a Broadway hit show." He writes that by partnering past masters with original music, "Chenoweth takes center stage with the kind of artful, witty numbers and the range of articulate emotions she would have been singing in Broadway's tuneful, show-stopping heyday, when joy, not disenchantment, was the musical's job description."

When performing the selections in concert, her challenge is to continue to make the work vocally pleasing but also to act out the story told in the songs. Singing, which she calls her second language, is how she learned to act anyway, since she always tried to tell the story of the song. Her vocal coach and mentor has described her as singing from her soul, not her ego. "I never want people to be aware of me as the singer," she says. "I want them to get lost in the song."

That ability to transform people with her singing, combined with her own comfort in front of an audience, makes her a natural for live performance. She returned to that world in the fall of 2001 after her series, *Kristin*, was canceled by NBC during the summer. Reviewing her performance in a City Center Encores! concert entitled "Broadway

Bash!" *New York Times* theatre critic Ben Brantley had this to say: "Ms. Chenoweth has been working to a laugh track in California. But the small screen doesn't begin to transmit her joyful intensity or talents. It's time to come home, Ms. Chenoweth."

She also performed for President George W. Bush twice— singing "A Spoonful of Sugar" for Julie Andrews at the 2001 "Kennedy Center Honors: A Celebration of the Performing Arts" and "The Girl in 14G," a song written for her CD by Jeanine Tesori and Dick Scanlon, at a benefit for Ford's Theatre in Washington, D.C.

Chenoweth sees comparisons between people getting lost in a song or play with the transformation people feel at worship. "I hear people say 'music is my religion' and 'theatre is my religion' and I understand." But for her God is always at the center, and she recognizes it is God's work at play when fans tell her they have been changed by her performances. "I believe we are given these gifts from God. It's the same thing that happens in worship, like a lightbulb going off, and you leave in peace."

Sometimes, though, people leave a play questioning. Then theatre has also done its job, she says. "I think God wants us to question, and not just accept. That's what theatre does, and so does worship."

For Casey Groves the transforming power of theatre works two ways. He has been so transformed by playing the role of Damien in Aldyth Morris's one-man play by that name that he is organizing a national tour to share with people the life of the Belgian-born priest who ministered to the lepers of the Hawaiian island Moloka'i. "A lot of times I'm a mess personally. But to play a character who brought so much life and light in the midst of much suffering helps me cultivate that kind of compassion. It makes my heart light."

Blessed Father Damien volunteered to go to the Hawaiian island in 1873 to care for the lepers who had been sent there by the government and, for the most part, abandoned. Father Damien's work became the foundation of a hospice movement worldwide, and because of his dedication to ministering to people with a lethal infectious disease, he has become the unofficial patron of people living with AIDS. Groves as Father Damien shares with the audience the intense suffering of those with "maggot-bloated sores" and how he copes "by remembering those worm-infested ulcers are the wounds of Christ."

"You can't get more real than that," Groves says. "It's a spur to action, to love better."

It gets so real that the transforming power reaches out to the audience and many people believe Groves is a priest in real life. After a performance at the Passionist monastery in Queens, New York, a priest excitedly shared his own missionary experiences with Groves. "He was talking to me like, 'You and I know.'"

Among those touched by a performance in the spring of 2002 at the Off-Broadway Jose Quintero Theatre was Howard E. Crouch, president of the Damien-Dutton Society for Leprosy, which provides funding for research, medical assistance, rehabilitation, education, and recreation for leprosy patients. He sent Groves a letter telling him he had captured Father Damien's moods, "a difficult task," and that Groves had brought to life much of his own writing on the life of Father Damien. He added a postscript: "I mean every word that I have written and your performance will live long in my memory. Good luck and God bless you."

That's the kind of reaction Groves loves, as any actor would. What he's uncomfortable with is when people identify him too much with Father Damien. Some almost confess to him after performances, telling him they're too lazy or that they don't love enough. After one show a young Franciscan friar with a group of friends waited until the others had left and he was alone with Groves. He told Groves he was preparing to take his final vows soon and that a section of the play in which Father Damien talks about temptation and how he kept his vow of celibacy had helped him. "He felt he could say this to me. It was a confession kind of moment."

Groves would rather people be a little less transformed.

"I find the social aspects of the play and his connection to God very earnest and powerful. I think he had a very high calling, but I'm just the actor. I'm not a priest and I feel a little weird about the responses I get. I'm not living on that island with all those lepers. I'm not making that sacrifice."

He's also not letting Father Damien take over his life, even though he has spent many hours trying to understand the priest to portray him fully. "I try not to connect in a general way. An actor has to create a sacred space. I feel it's wise to let go or it could affect me psychologically." He has, though, imagined conversations with Father Damien before performances. "I imagine he says, 'Don't worry so much. You're doing fine.' Then I let him go." Letting a character become too involving offstage is dangerous. "I could play any kind of character. If I open the door to one character, how do I decide what door to open? I could be building a habit."

But he does keep aware of Father Damien's spirit. "I don't want to get too weird, but I feel he's with me, guarding me. I do feel blessed when I do it."

Stage and film actor Lesley Collis feels blessed as a performer, but also in one of her offstage roles—that of lector, or lay reader, at St. Malachy's. She shared her experience one afternoon, sitting in the living room of her theatre district apartment, sipping a mug of tea. "Something amazing happens when I'm lectoring, which I take very seriously and take great joy in doing. I have to center myself; it's not a theatre performance. I study ahead of time and I pray about it. Then I walk up and stand and look at the words as if I'm seeing them for the very first time."

Even though she has read the scripture passage at home and in the sacristy right before Mass, it becomes new as she reads to the congregation. "The most amazing feeling comes over me, like I'm being transformed. Even though I've rehearsed at home, I find new meaning and ways of coloring, new beats and nuances. The Holy Spirit just takes over. I can physically feel it. It just runs through me. I get such a sense of peace. I'm getting shivers just thinking of it."

When she finishes the passage she says the prescribed ending, "The Word of the Lord," and "it's almost as if I step off of a ledge of reality. When I say 'The Word of the Lord' it's me. Sometimes I've stood there and just been in awe. It happens every single time. I literally don't know who's up there." As an actor, she's used to being before an audience, but this is different. "I'm so in tune when I perform. I have that comfort level. This is almost like an out-of-body experience."

She remembers being especially blown away by reading St. Paul's famous letter to the Corinthians about love: "If I speak in the tongues of mortals and of angels, but do not have love, I am a noisy gong or a clanging cymbal. . . . Love is patient; love is kind. . . . It does not insist on its own way. . . . It bears all things, believes all things, hopes all things, endures all things." "I was transformed and transfixed by those words. I felt like they were running out of my pores."

She is acutely aware that what she is reading as a lector is in a separate category from anything she says onstage as an actor. "It's not a performance; it's the word of the Lord. It's not being up there to give glory to me, it's to give glory to God's word. That's a big responsibility. It's awesome."

Just as reading the word of the Lord at St. Malachy's is a transforming experience for her, so was her journey to that particular church. Telling it brings tears to her eyes, for it is a story she has shared with few people.

Collis, whose family was not religious, grew up in England, moving frequently because her father, a baker, kept getting transferred.

Mostly the family lived on the south coast, with her grade school years spent in Sussex where she attended the school of St. George's Cathedral. It was very high Church of England and Collis loved it. She sang in the choir and was involved in many extracurricular religious activities. "Bible study classes were very important to me. I didn't have to be persuaded to go." She also didn't have to be persuaded to go to church on Sunday or during the week, for that matter. Since the cathedral was right next to her school, she visited frequently. "For me to be in church is such a luxury. I'd spend all my time in church if I could. I love visiting churches."

Then for a time when she was older, she stopped going; but when she went back, "I came back with a vengeance."

This is what happened. She was staying with a friend in Scottsdale, Arizona, when she felt the urge to go to church after having not done so in about five years. She mentioned it to her friend and was surprised to learn her friend was a practicing Roman Catholic who said she would be happy to take Lesley to her church, St. Maria Goretti.

The following Sunday Collis accompanied her friend, casually entering the church with no expectations. She didn't know her life would be changed by going through those doors. "I walked into Maria Goretti and it was as if I had been hit. It was a physical force. My friend couldn't get over it. Tears poured down my face and I wept through the service like a faucet. It was the most unbelievably strong emotion. I didn't know what hit me, but it was real." Collis, who was having family problems at the time, believes she was led to St. Maria Goretti by the Blessed Mother, who many believe makes visitations to the church. "I needed a mother."

Feeling a desire to connect more deeply with this Mother, she attended a Marian convention and "was totally blown away by everything." When she returned to New York, she began "a two-year mission" in search of a Catholic church, attending Masses and, in some cases, returning more than once to various churches. "It was almost like a crusade. I searched long and hard."

Although she had grown up in the Anglican Church, which in this country is the Episcopal Church, she believes the Blessed Mother had sent her a sign calling her to Catholicism. It happened shortly after she returned from the Marian convention, at Holy Cross Catholic Church on West Forty-second Street in Manhattan. She had been going there daily for two weeks to pray and meditate in the Blessed Mother's chapel. One afternoon while she was praying the rosary at the altar rail, the round pewter medal of the Crucifixion she had been holding "jumped out of my hand" and fell not far from where she was kneeling. She saw it, but didn't want to stop praying. When she finished her rosary, she looked to the spot where the medal had fallen, but the medal was gone. She got down on all fours and searched the marble floor, but couldn't find it. What she did find after much searching was a medal with St. Maria Goretti on the front and the inscription "Pray for us" on the back. She had been alone in the church the whole time. "It's the Blessed Mother. She sent me a sign. I had a direct call, as far as I'm concerned, to be a Catholic and committed."

She began in earnest searching for a Catholic parish. "St. Malachy's found me. I must have passed by a hundred times but never went in. One day I was walking by not even thinking, when I stopped dead in my tracks. I went in and that was it. I had such a gut feeling that was very, very profound. I just knew."

She is now seriously considering being received into the Catholic Church, and she carries the St. Maria Goretti medal with her everywhere.

With her theatre background, she feels at home at St. Malachy's. "I love the liturgy, the ceremonial aspect. We've lost that in life. I have that feeling in the theatre. The theatre is a sacred space, a temple. When I'm working in a theatre I'm respectful of the place. I have a sense of responsibility to the place and the audience and the art. That transformation is similar, it's secular, but we are still creating a sacred space. I always pray first, asking that I might give glory to God through my performance, that he will work through me to touch hearts and that I'll utilize the gifts he's given me honorably."

She's the first to arrive and the last to leave. "I always go out on the stage and stand and soak it in. If I can do it, this is where I will pray. You just don't get that on a film set. It's a totally different space. It's mechanical and cold. The big thing is there's no audience. You're not sharing. You don't touch hearts immediately."

She has that same sense of reverence for a sacred space when she's in the audience. "Walking into the theatre is like walking into church. It's quiet, I settle down, then my heart starts beating when the actors come out and are there with the audience. It's like church coming alive with the people. The spirit moves. We become a company, with everybody joining together in a mutual experience. We become one body."

For Shoshana Bean, that sense of communal transformation has come through her involvement with Broadway Inspirational Voices. "I just love gospel music and always have, good little Jewish girl that I am. I have no idea why. I've always been a huge fan. I was raised in a household with diverse music—blues, jazz, gospel, and rhythm & blues."

That household, in Portland, Oregon, was also a religious Jewish one, but seeds were planted there and shortly after Bean hit New York City in 1999, she sought out a place in a gospel choir. Now she's singing verses like "Everywhere I go, everywhere I be, Jesus is mine" and "My life was full of sin, Jesus washed my soul within. Since Jesus purified my soul, I will rejoice he's made me whole."

While that's not exactly standard fare for a good little Jewish girl, the transformational experience of singing in the choir is more important to Bean than the words she is singing. Besides, her comfort in dealing with Jesus had already been eased by having performed in the thirtieth-anniversary Off-Broadway production of

Godspell in 2000. As a graduate of the University of Cincinnati College Conservatory of Music, she appreciates the opportunity—and challenge—of singing gospel music.

"It's beyond 'Jesus is mine.' That doesn't mean anything to me. I know I don't pray to that God and I still hold to my beliefs. It's the chords, the clapping of hands, that spirit, that energy. That's hard to hold in this world."

That power helps bridge the Jewish–Christian barrier, Bean says. It works for her and for her parents, who traveled from Oregon in 2001 to hear the choir's annual fall fundraising concert and loved it. Still her mother said: "You're not going to convert, are you?" Bean says she would "never go to that extreme. I'm rooted in Passover seders. I'm still culturally rooted in Judaism, but I can be inspired by a lot of other things."

Her Jewish practices were more a part of her life when she was a child and went to Sunday and Wednesday school and Hebrew school. "Three days a week were taken up with Judaism." She felt closest to her faith while studying for her bat mitzvah and in the years following because she understood the prayers and could say them on a deeper level. She slacked off a bit in high school, but began thinking about her faith again in college. "I realized now it's my responsibility to be Jewish. I wanted to go to services and light candles on Friday night."

In the hectic pace of New York performing life, where she made her Broadway debut in August 2002 in *Hairspray*, she doesn't keep to the rituals as much, but still considers herself "a spiritual, God-centered person. I forgive myself if I don't light the candles, but not if I'm not God-centered," she says, adding that singing in the choir has helped. "Through the choir a sense of spirituality has awakened in me that I didn't know was possible."

That keeps her focused in a showbiz world which included, at twenty-four, opening in a critically and commercially successful musical. "I'm so blessed I get paid to do this, coming to work when this is where I work and not a restaurant."

Being cast in *Hairspray* meant she didn't have to turn to restaurant work in her foreseeable future. Based on John Waters's 1988 movie, the show follows a young white girl's attempts to integrate a television dance show in 1962 Baltimore, which only allows blacks in once a month for Negro Day. Even though technical problems struck on opening night of the Seattle tryouts, forcing the show to stop after the first number and restart five minutes later, *Daily Variety Gotham* critic Lynn Jacobson said it took her only two scenes to realize the creators "have a shiny new hit on their hands." Critics fell over themselves celebrating the "glorious Technicolor sets," costumes, and hair (naturally), as well as the singing, high-energy dancing, and music.

In New York, more great praise followed, with Bean's efforts in the chorus being praised communally. Ben Brantley, reviewing the show for the *New York Times*, said director Jack O'Brien "has made sure that none of his ensemble members—who include the freshest array of young singers and dancers since *Rent*—keep even an inch of distance from their material." Bean's performance was singled out two months later when Shirley MacLaine went backstage after a show and told her she was a shining light onstage and predicted she would be a star.

Bean played Shelley, a teen dancer on the show, and understudied the lead. Even though religion wasn't a part of the show, Bean brought her Judaism to bear. Since little was mentioned about Shelley, she gave her an imaginary identity in which she was Jewish, but didn't want anyone on the TV show to find out for fear she would be thrown off.

She certainly doesn't have that fear about Broadway Inspirational Voices. And even though singing about Jesus is a stretch from her background, it provides her with a wider musical outlet than she found in Judaism, which she says left her few choices. "Being musically centered is what heals me. It's opening up body and mouth and letting something out that is beyond words. The style takes over. There's power in gospel music to bring healing. It's spiritually inspiring."

Bean's experience of communal transformation is central to Judaism, and so is the personal transformation path she follows. Rabbi Richard Jacobs, senior rabbi of Westchester Reform Temple in Scarsdale, New York, says the personal journey is the core of Jewish practice. "It means I'm evolving and growing and not who I'm ultimately going to be. We're put on this planet with a certain kind of path. Following that is backbreaking spiritual work, which takes practice and discipline."

The quest for personal transformation is most evident during the High Holy Days, he says, when special things are asked of Jews. He cites the Hebrew expression *cheshbon hanefesh*, which means an accounting of the soul. "We look deeply at our lives and heal that which we have broken to prepare ourselves for the new year." This healing, *teshuvah*, could mean calling someone you have hurt to try to repair the relationship. "That's the core work of what we do."

Jacobs has a response for young congregation members when they associate Rosh Hashanah with the time to blow the shofar. "I say, 'It's the time to work on yourself.' The really important work of Judaism is to refine ourselves, to climb the proverbial Jacob's ladder of refinement."

He points to a current trend in Judaism that emphasizes institutional reform, but he believes people need to get back to the basic work of personal transformation. "Synagogues should not be places that offer lots of programs. They should help you grow deeper into who you are and strengthen your relationship with God and others. Ultimately our tradition is to transform the world. The pain and injustice of our world demand we not just rise above it but work to change it, to transform the world into the one God envisioned, to be coworkers with God in creating that universe."

A good biblical example of personal transformation, Jacobs says, is found in Genesis with Jacob, "the embodiment of the transformed soul." Jacob deceives his father to receive the blessing meant for his brother, Esau, then goes off to his kinsman, Laban, to find a wife. "Jacob is a slippery character; you've got to watch him with both eyes," Jacobs says. On the journey, he dreams of a ladder going from earth to heaven with the angels of God ascending and descending on it. "His dream is a metaphor for his own life. He's struggling mightily to lift himself from his behavior. His transformation comes with a lot of pain."

That pain occurs when he experiences deception after Laban tricks him into seven years of service with the promise of marriage to his daughter Rachel, only to unite him with his other daughter, Leah. After seven more years of service, Jacob is allowed to marry Rachel as well, but he doesn't live happily ever after. He experiences more pain and deception after his sons sell his favorite son, Joseph, into slavery and tell him Joseph has been killed. But Jacob grows through his trials. God changes his name to Israel, which means "one who struggles with beings divine and human and prevails," and he becomes the founder of a nation. "At the end in his complete transformation as patriarch he's been refined by his life's experiences, his painful life experiences." Jacobs likes the story of Jacob because "you can watch him change before your eyes."

In his own life, Jacobs has found transformation in traditional ways like prayer and liturgies but also in dance. Growing up in California he liked to dance, but it wasn't something boys did, except at school affairs. So when he went to the University of California at Santa Barbara he majored in comparative religion and drama, which fed his performance interest. After graduation he spent six years as a dancer and choreographer with the Avodah Dance Ensemble, a modern dance company that performs Jewish services in dance and concerts throughout the United States. He also has led workshops on movement and prayer at Hebrew Union College (where he was ordained in 1982), Union Theological Seminary, and other settings.

While with the Avodah Dance Ensemble, he learned to explore Jewish spirituality through movement, conducting entire sabbath services through dance, sometimes with traditional music woven in. "It changed how I thought of prayer," Jacobs says. "It's been a huge part of my development." It led him into the doctoral program in ritual dance at New York University, where he studied the role of dance in different religions.

"The artist is the closest thing to a person who can create a language that is nonverbal and transcends to a deeper level. We can be so analytical in Western religions. We need to tap into a deeper plane, to get outside the verbal. That's the way we enter into the world of the holy, nonrational, and artistic. It's a window of prayer."

The Rev. William A. Doubleday also has given a great deal of thought to transformation, as an Episcopal priest contemplating the teachings of his Christian faith and as a professor of pastoral theology at New York's General Theological Seminary. "Any kind of major change of mood or insight or commitment could be transformational. It's a radical change in some significant part of one's life. That change could be a new beginning or a profound insight. It's turning over a new leaf." Sometimes sadness prompts the transformation. "People with some experience of death, loss, grief, or disappointment can come to a new beginning."

The change also can spring from something that has nothing to do with someone's own circumstances. "A person can go to a play or musical and come out significantly different, for a few minutes or a lifetime." For him, transformation happens during Rodgers and Hammerstein's musicals. "They are an utterly uplifting experience. You leave with some sense of hope in the human spirit and potential."

The transformation that comes into play in Christianity is grounded in a commitment to social change by bringing the gospel values of love, truth, and justice to bear on the culture, Doubleday says. "That's what the life of the faith community is all about." This means not just believing in the Kingdom of God but also working to create glimpses of that Kingdom in the here and now. "Christianity is essentially a very social religion. In our liturgy we pray for the whole state of Christ's Church in the world and we pray for our enemies too. At the exchange of peace we reach out and touch and greet not just our friends but strangers too."

One can achieve the personal transformation that feeds into this by developing spiritual practices like meditation, prayer, and scripture reading, Doubleday says. "Be attentive to scripture and tradition. Listen to the word and engage in the word." And remember that the pursuit of transformation should be ongoing. "Christians need to have a sense of being on a journey and pilgrimage. When we are aware of this, we become more attuned to the world around us on our journey and God's blessed role in the changes of our lives. Even when the change is in the midst of suffering or disappointment, grace breaks in and brings a new beginning." This journeying involves a commitment to vocation, not just as in ordination but in a sense of being called. "Every Christian has a vocation to live out the Christian life in the world."

That vocation is rooted in the Baptismal Covenant, which adults say at their baptism, parents and godparents say on behalf of an infant at baptism, and Christians renew at various times, such as in witnessing a baptism. It asks the basic questions of the faith, such as whether one believes in God the Father; Jesus Christ, the Son of God; and God the Holy Spirit. These questions are followed by what Doubleday calls "the action clause": "Will you continue in the apostles' teaching and fellowship, in the breaking of bread, and in the prayers?" The answer is "I will, with God's help."

The next question deals with repentance and ethical and moral living, recognizing that no human being is perfect. "Will you persevere in resisting evil, and, whenever you fall into sin, repent and return to the Lord?" The question implies the ongoing work of personal transformation, Doubleday says. "In sermons I say the Church is a hospital for sinners, not a museum for holy relics."

The final two questions deal with the social/relational dimension of transformation. "Will you seek and serve Christ in all persons, loving your neighbor as yourself?" and "Will you strive for justice and peace among all people, and respect the dignity of every human being?" In responding to these questions the Episcopal Church has been "radically transformed in the last four or five decades," Doubleday says, citing the ordination of women, respect for gay and lesbian Christians, and the fight against racism. This emphasis on social transformation is so essential, Christianity couldn't exist without it. "It's running throughout the gospels. It's a kind of turning-the-world-upside-down theme."

That is the mission he tries to instill in his students at General Seminary, the oldest Episcopal seminary. "I work with students to attempt to open up new possibilities for ministry, not to re-create the mythical Church of the 1950s. We're called to do something new in the twenty-first century."

Looking for new ways to get the message across, Doubleday assigns classic literature, contemporary novels, and plays. At one point he required his first-year seminarians to see *Les Misérables* on Broadway. "It's a profoundly theological work. The conflict between works and grace is what it's all about. The released prisoner did something wrong, but his life is all about love and caring for others. He's relentlessly pursued by Javert, the embodiment of rigidity, the embodiment of the law. In the end grace wins out, but some lovely people suffer and die on the way. Do we live strictly by rules or a gospel of love in which we look anew at someone?"

Doubleday says that message of transforming love is at the heart of the three defining events of Christianity—the Incarnation, the Crucifixion, and the Resurrection. In the Incarnation, Christians believe God became human in the person of Jesus Christ. Doubleday quotes from the Magnificat, the prayer Mary says after she is told by the angel Gabriel that she has been chosen to be the mother of the Savior: "He has cast down the mighty from their thrones, and has lifted up the lowly. He has filled the hungry with good things, and the rich he has sent away empty." The message is of social change. "Mary speaks transformational words," he says.

For the Crucifixion, Doubleday reads from the Good Friday service in *The Book of Common Prayer*, the Episcopal prayer book: "Let the whole world see and know that things which were cast down are being raised up, and things which had grown old are being made new, and that all things are being brought to their perfection by him through whom all things were made, your Son Jesus Christ our Lord; who lives and reigns with you, in the unity of the Holy Spirit, one God, for ever and ever."

And finally, the transformation of Easter: "The resurrection event is the ultimate comment on turning the world upside down. That which was dead is alive. In essence, a belief in the resurrection is the deep conviction that no glimpse of death, grief, loss, or failure in our lives is the end of the story in either human or divine terms. "

Photograph by Merwin Goldsmith

About the Author

R ETTA BLANEY is a theatre and religion writer in Manhattan. Her work has appeared in the *Washington Post, New York Newsday, National Catholic Reporter, The Jewish Week, The Living Church, American Theatre, Back Stage*, and other publications. She is editor of the anthology *Journalism Stories from the Real World*, a collection of essays for which Walter Cronkite wrote the introduction, and has taught at Brooklyn College, New York University, and Marymount Manhattan College.

As a full-time reporter, she worked for newspapers in Maryland and New York, winning a half dozen reporting awards.

She holds a master of arts in modern drama from New York University, a master of fine arts in playwriting from Brooklyn College, and a bachelor of arts in English from the College of Notre Dame of Maryland.

She is founder and coordinator of Broadway Blessing, an interfaith service of song and scripture reading that brings the theatre community together every September to ask God's blessing on the new season, and is an associate member of the Sisters of Charity of New York.